"Enchanted Forest: A Woodland Coloring Adventure"

is delighted to welcome you. This coloring book is intended to transport you to a mystical forest teeming with intriguing animals and hidden surprises. When you turn the pages, you'll come across gorgeous deer, powerful wolves, and majestic lions, all set in a stunning woodland environment that will pique your interest and transport you to another planet.

With each page flip, you'll uncover fresh surprises, such as twisting vines and shimmering streams, as well as hidden passages that encourage you to go further into this enchanting woodland. When you color in these beautiful pictures, you'll become lost in the intricacies and lost in your own thoughts, lost in a fascinating and enchanting universe.

This coloring book is ideal for relaxing and destressing after a long day, connecting into your creative side, and losing yourself in a world of beauty and wonder. Now grab your pencils, choose your colors, and let your imagination soar as you go on this forest coloring adventure.

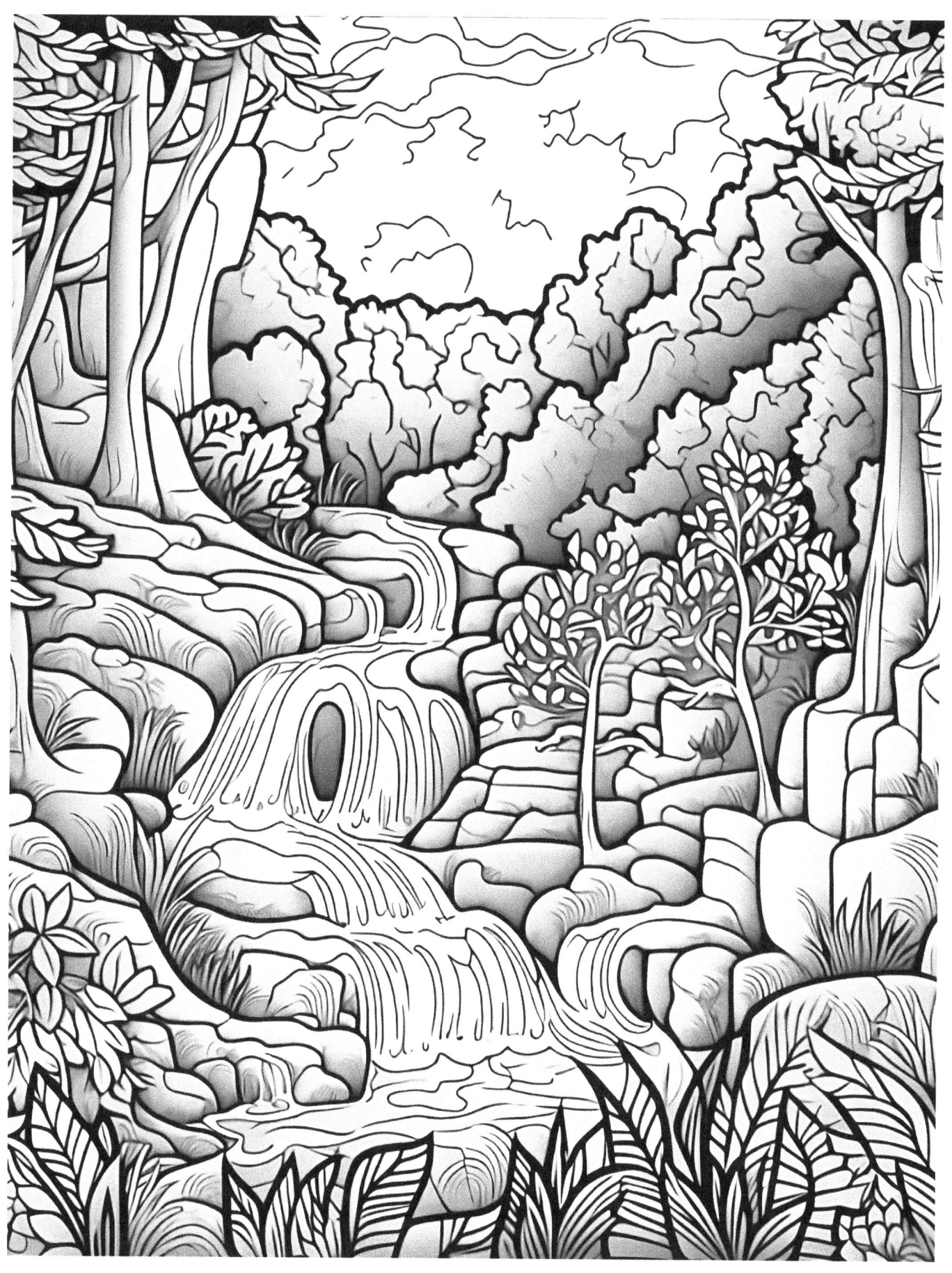

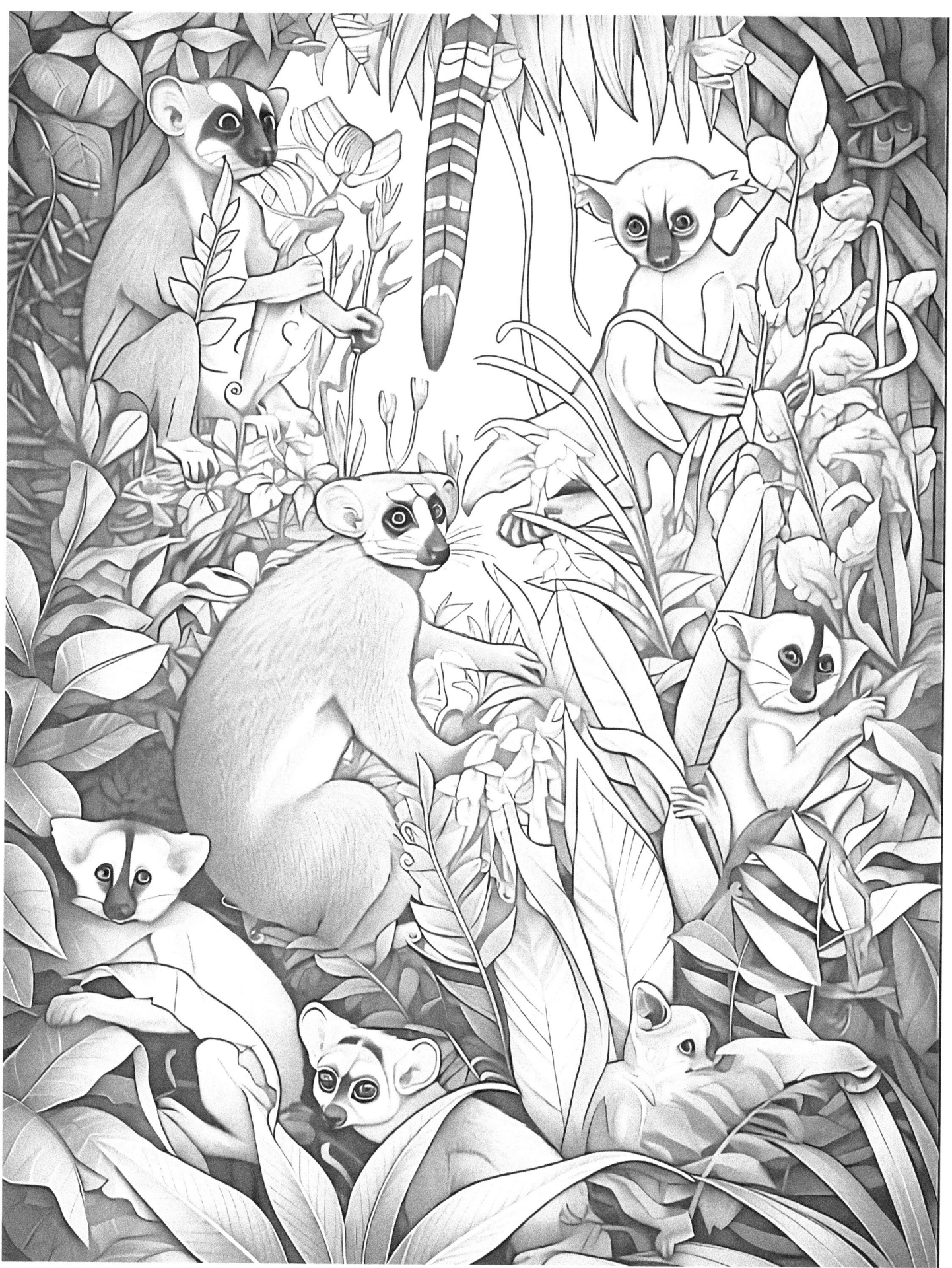

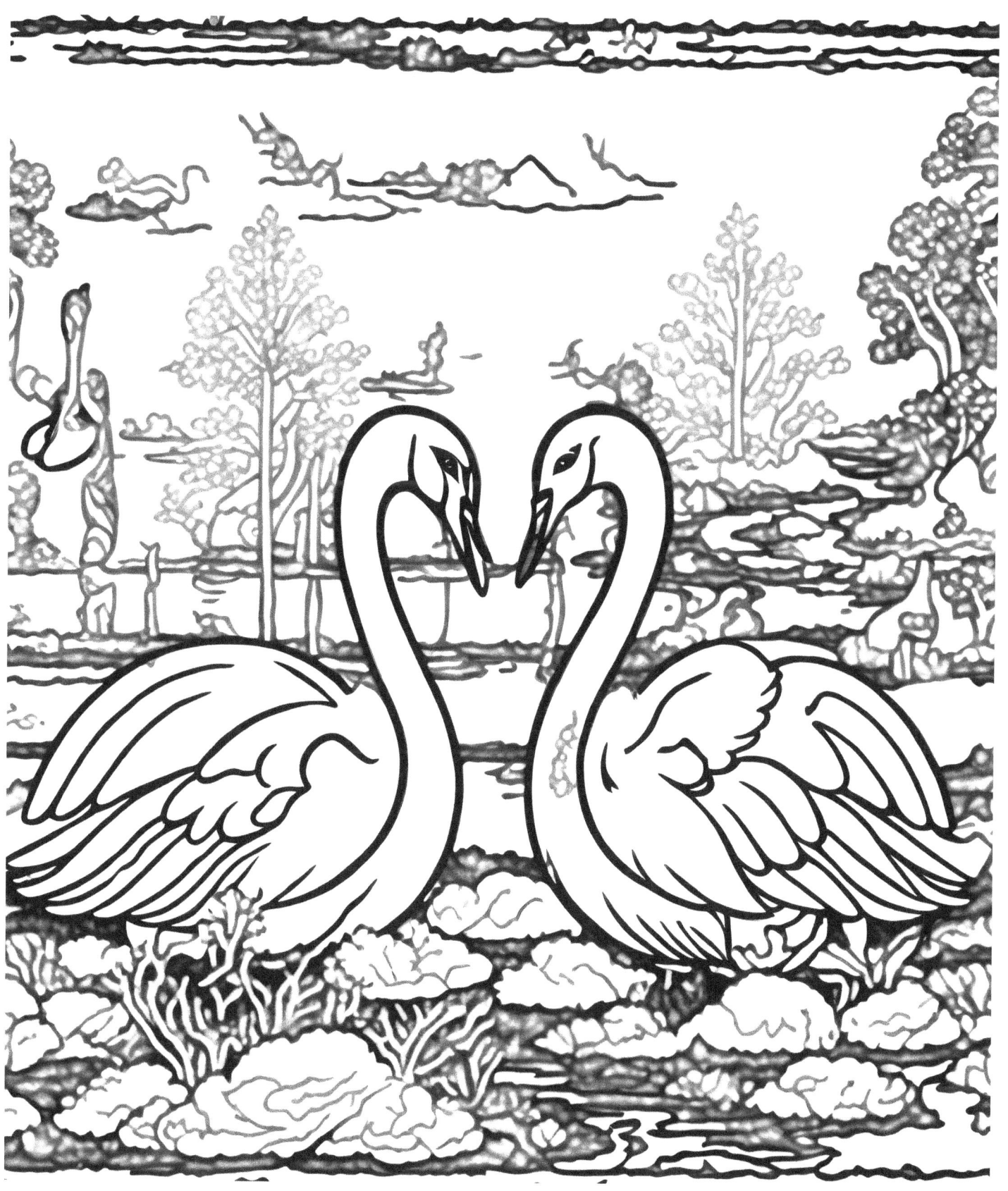

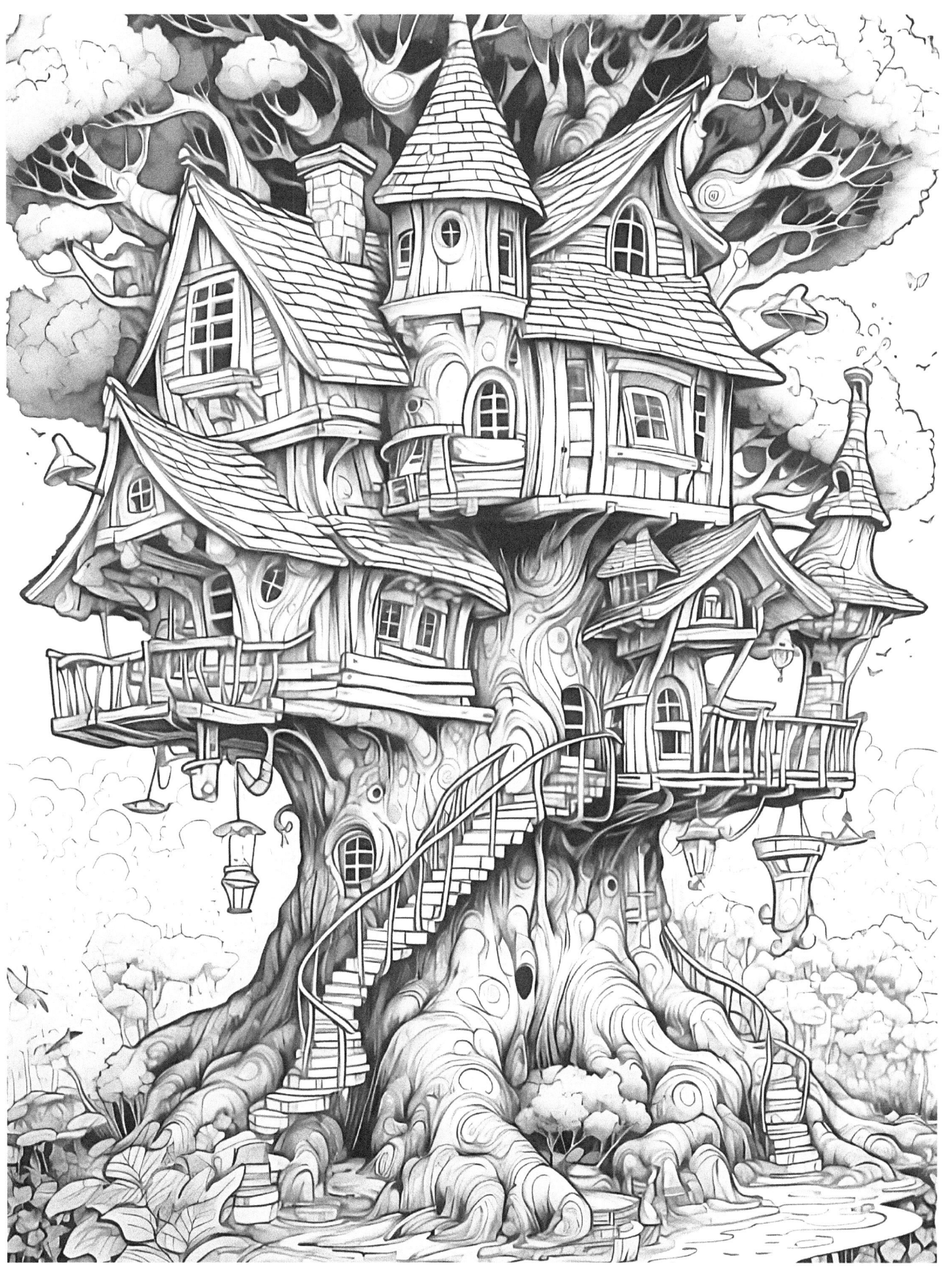

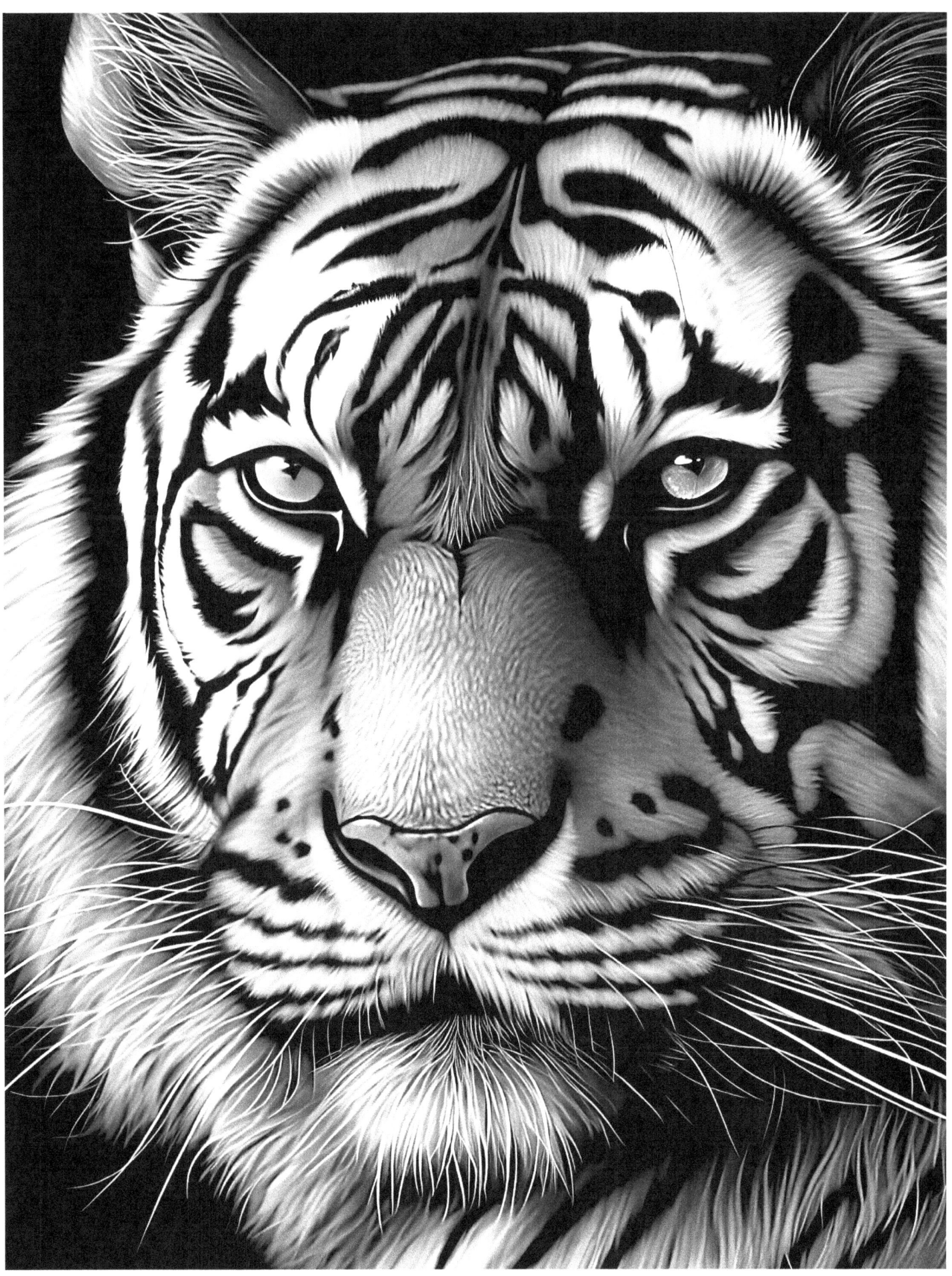

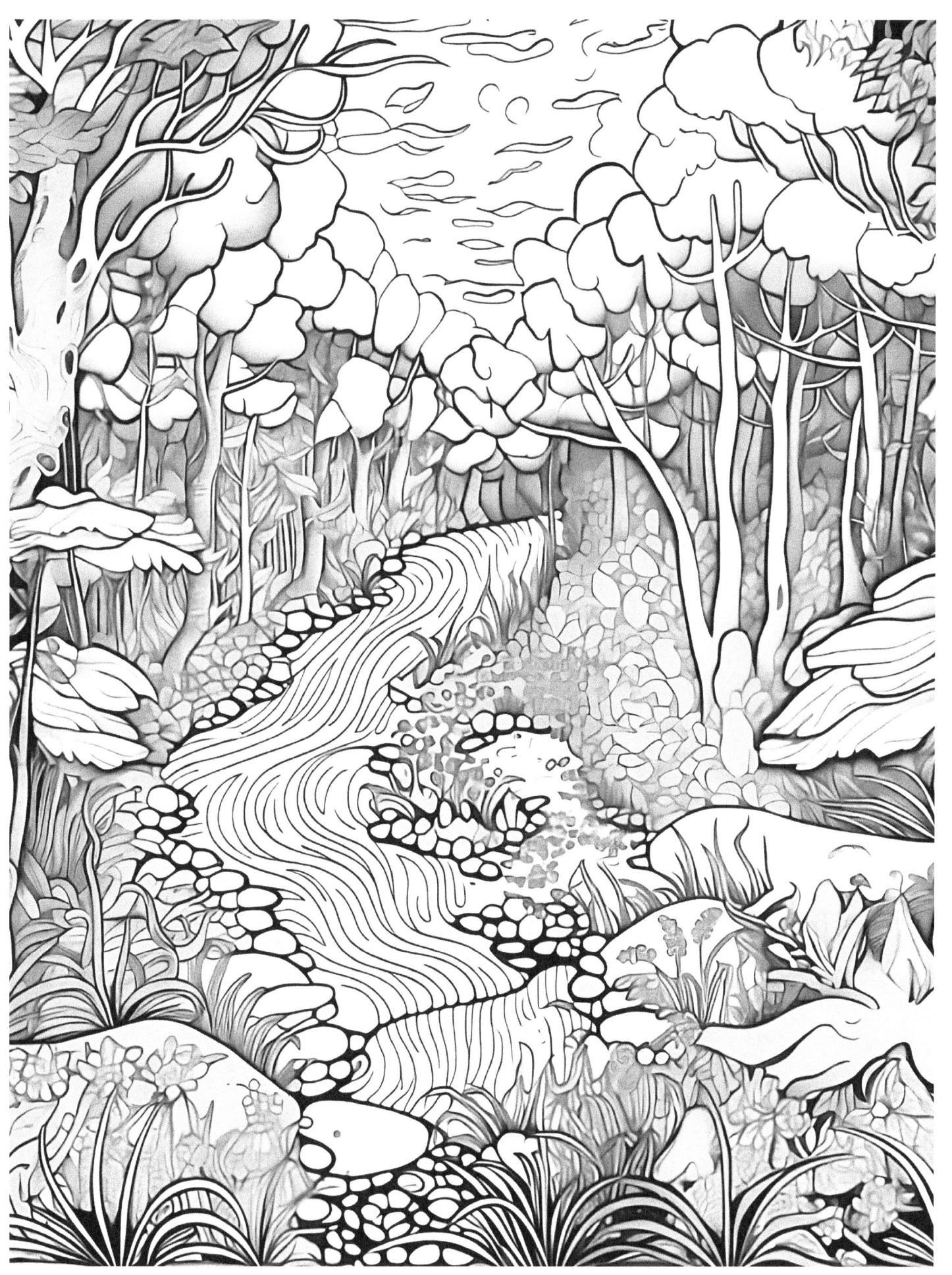

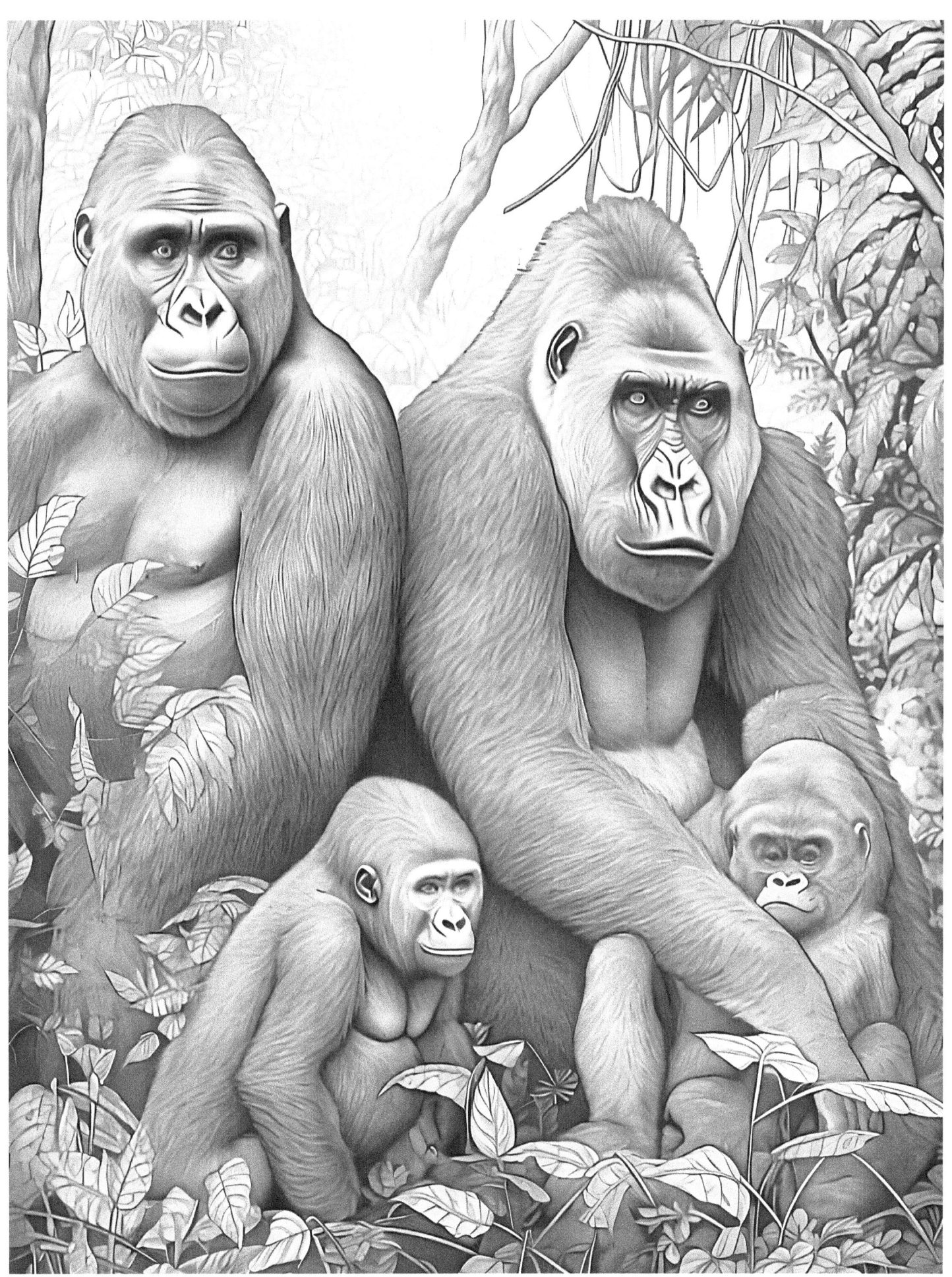

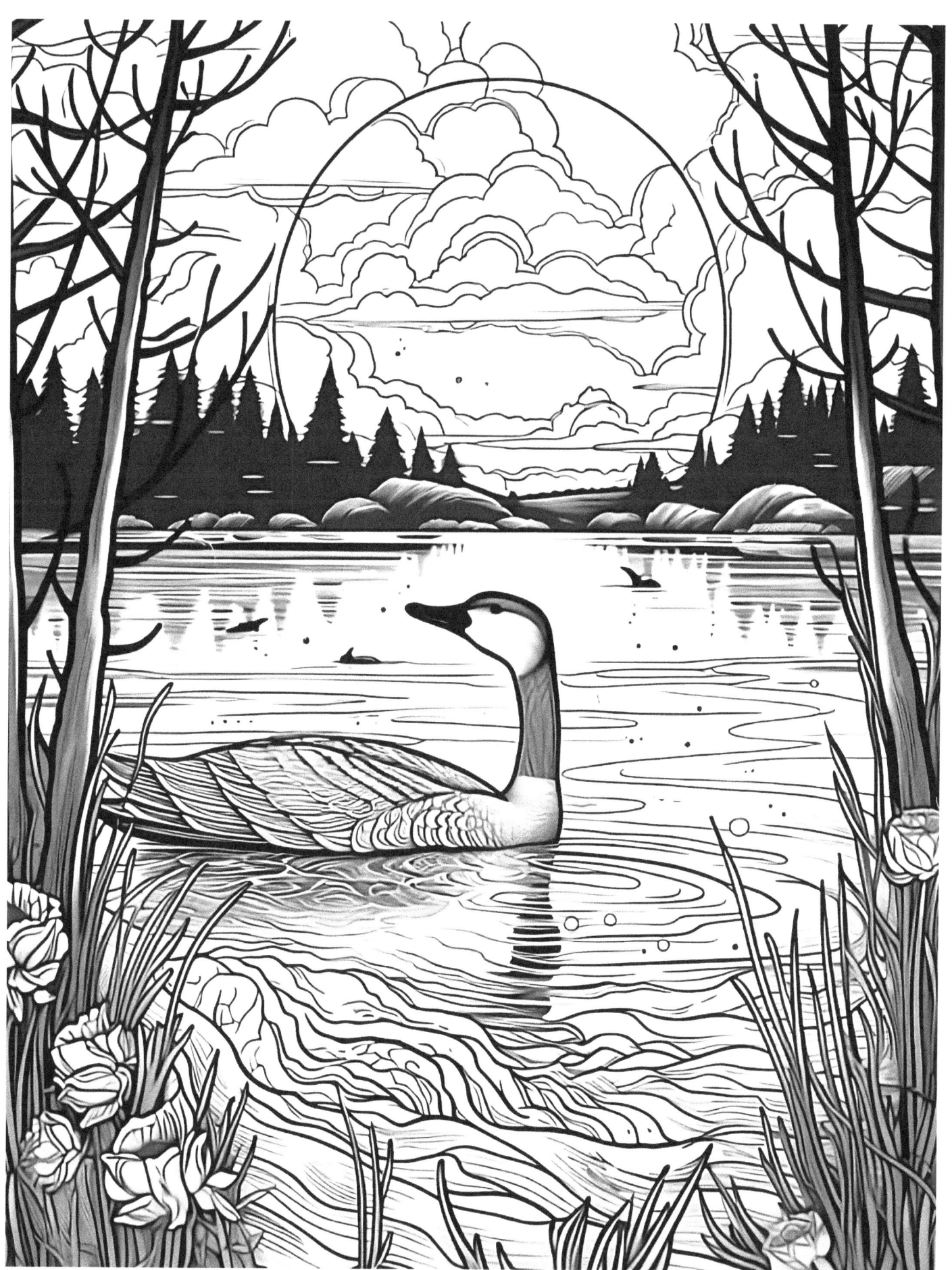

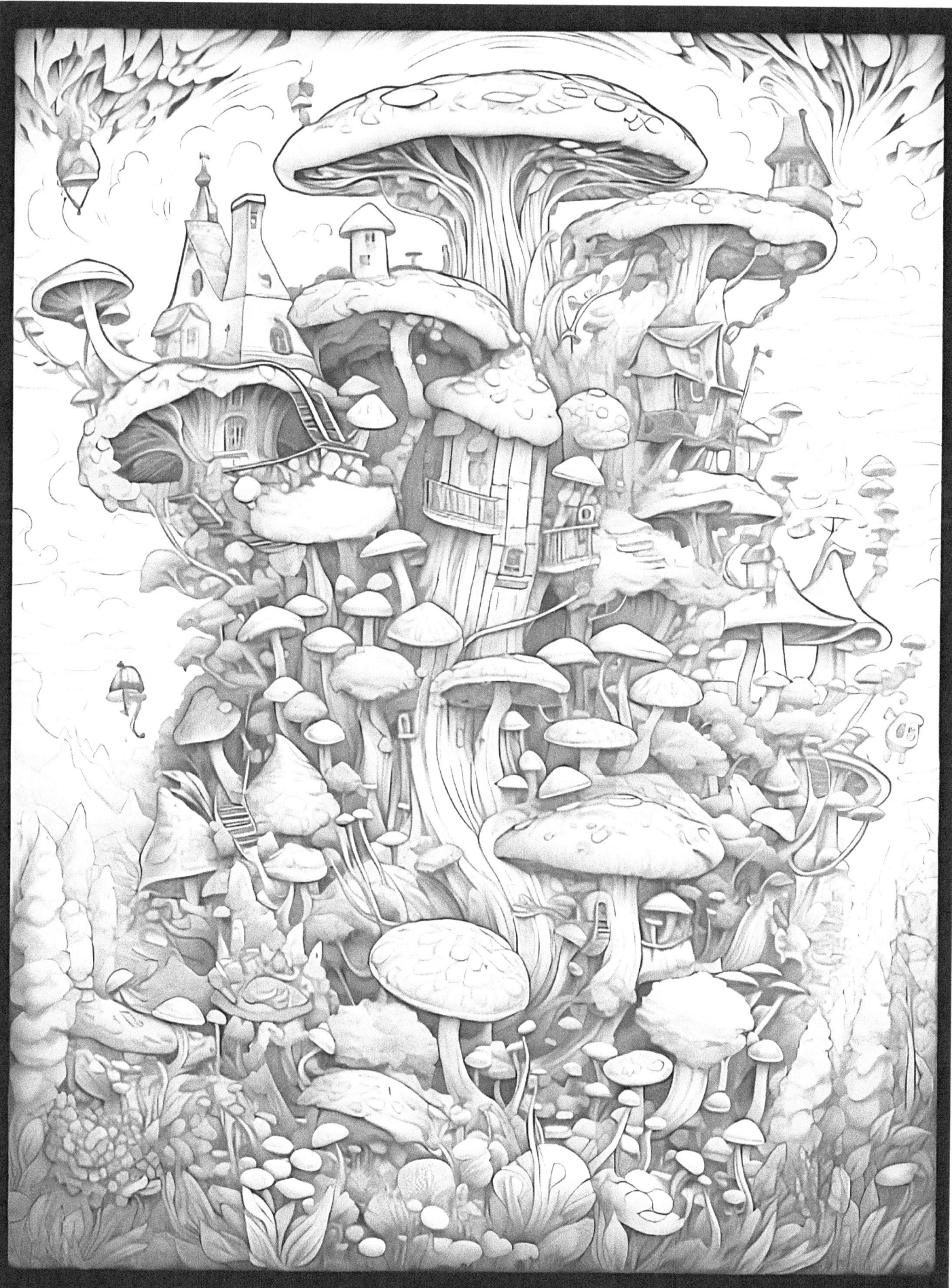

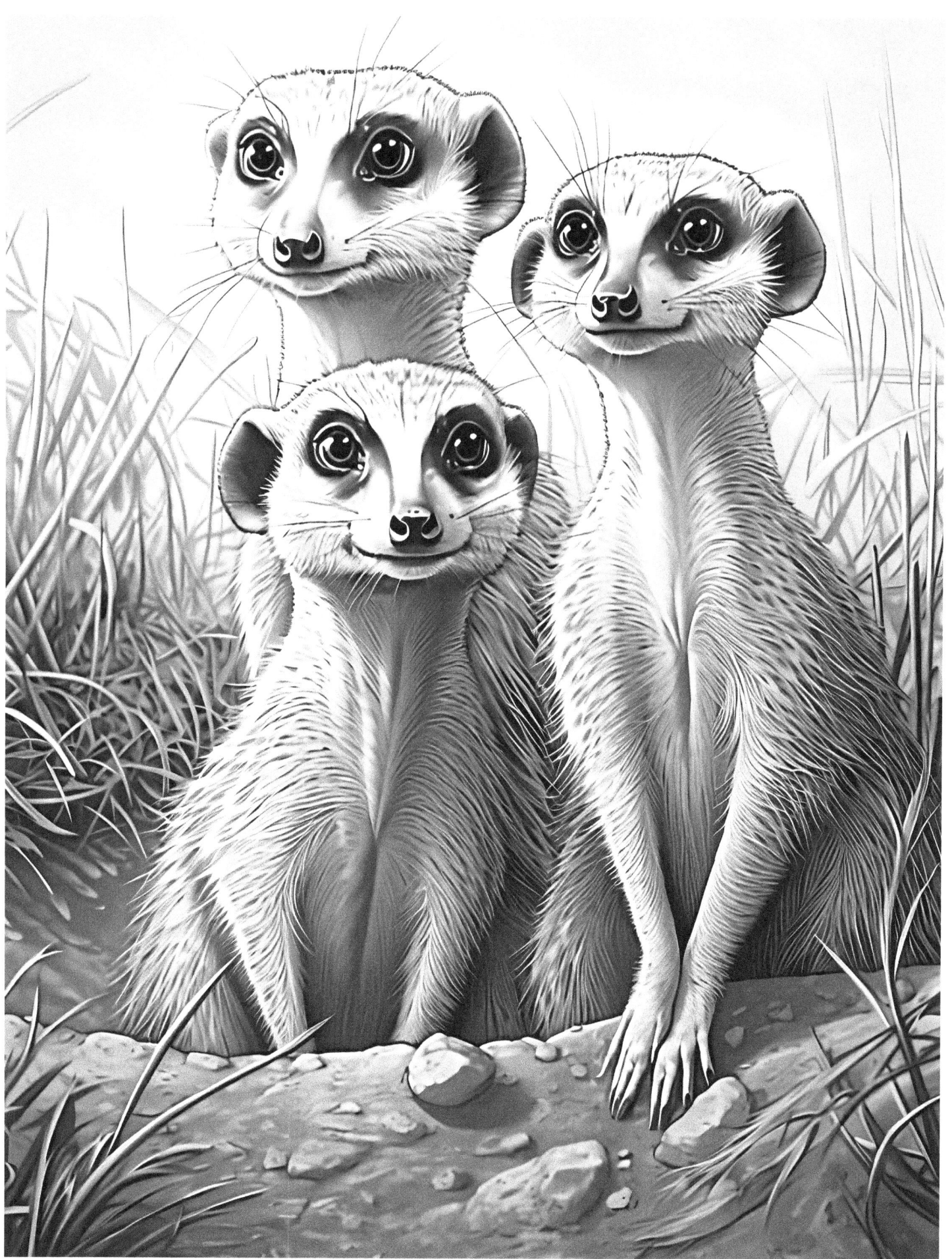

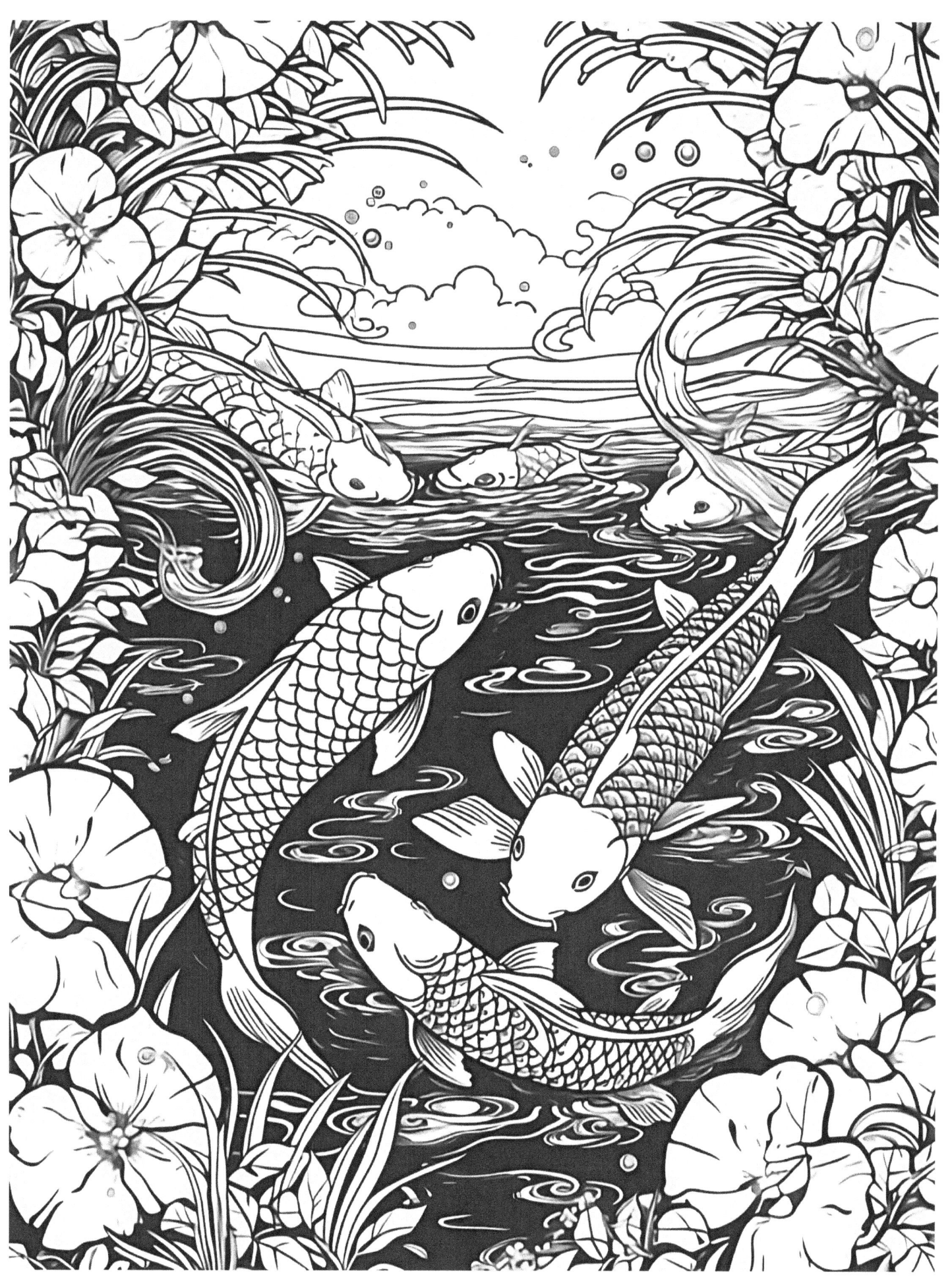

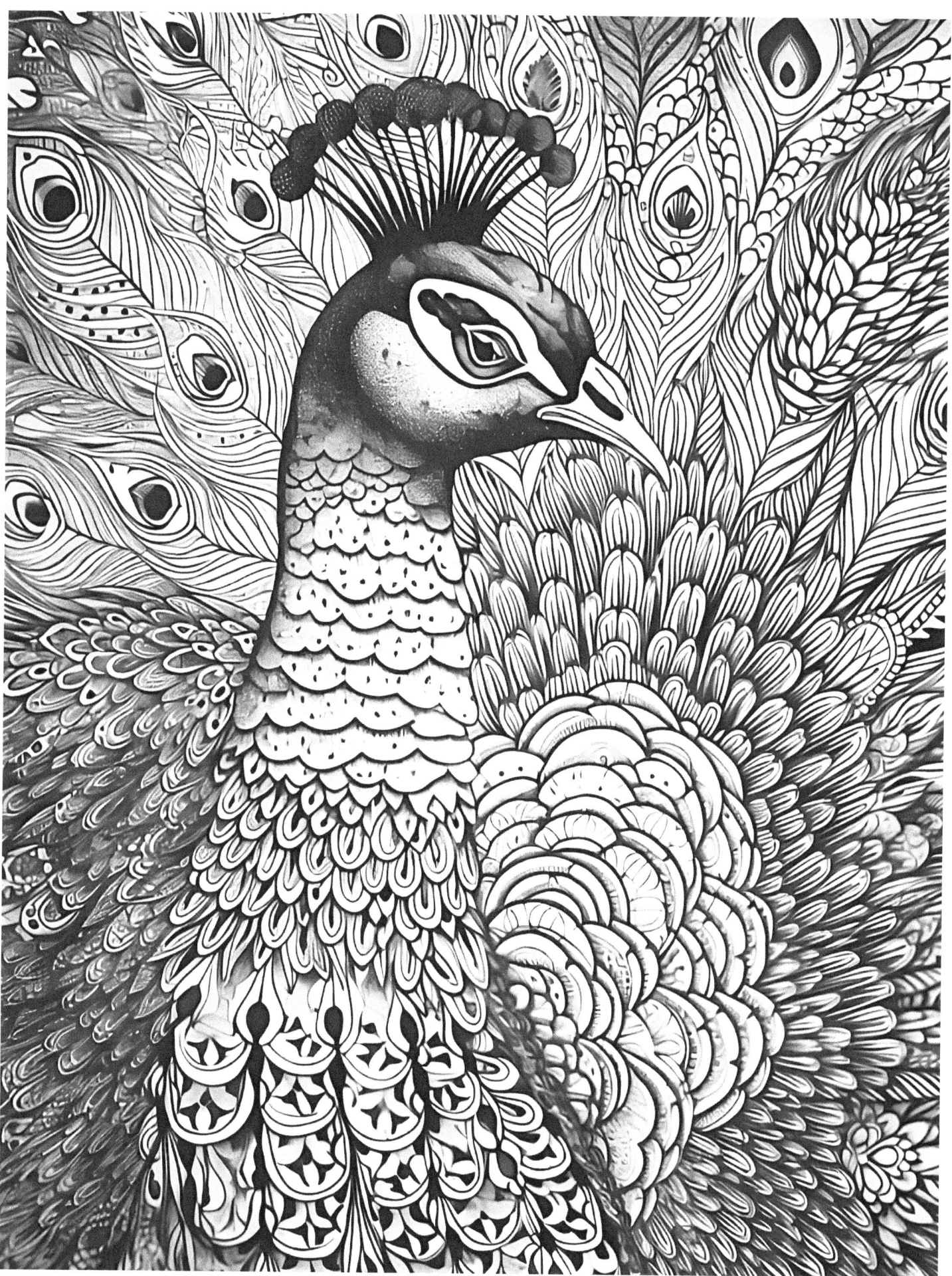

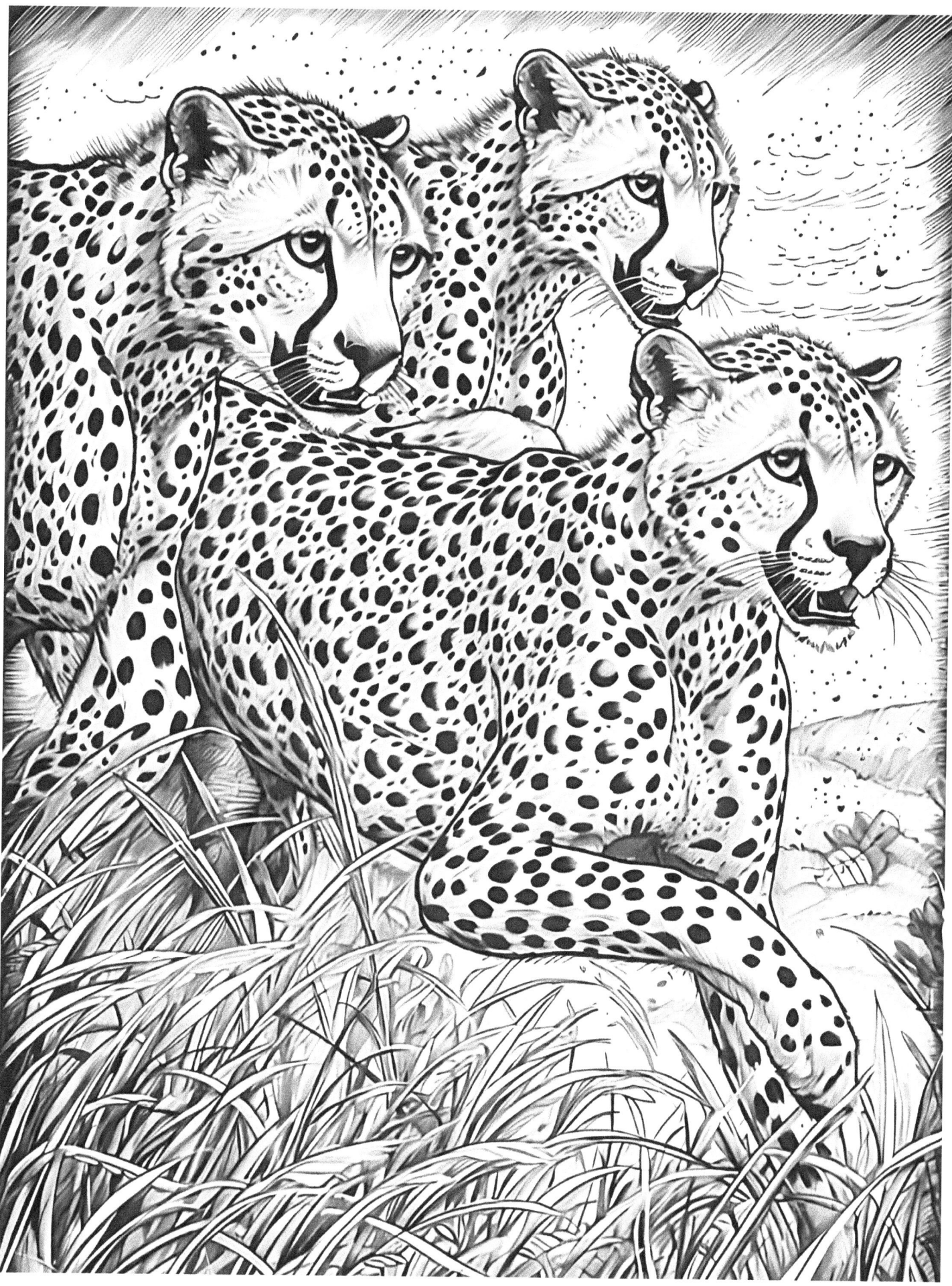

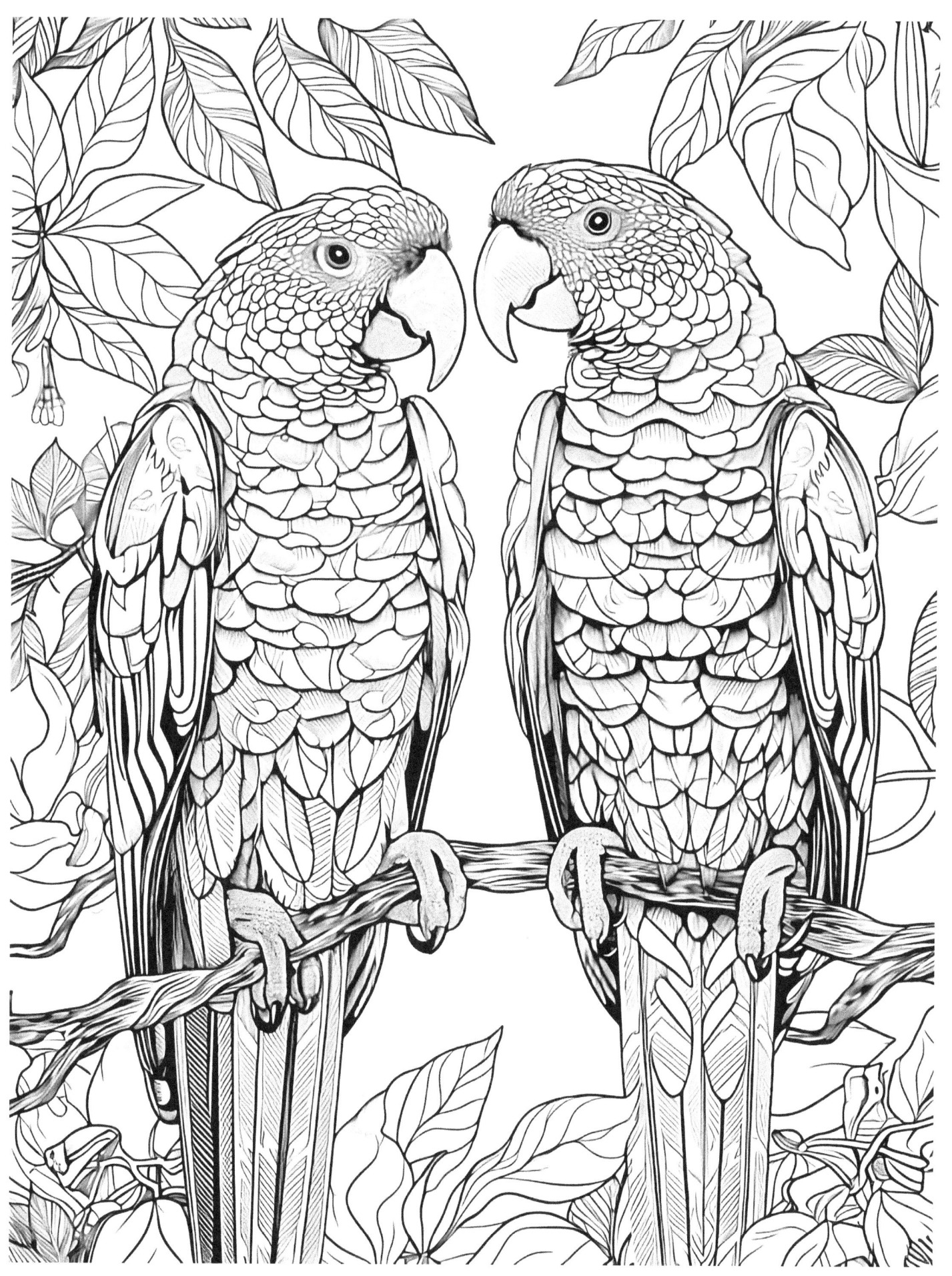

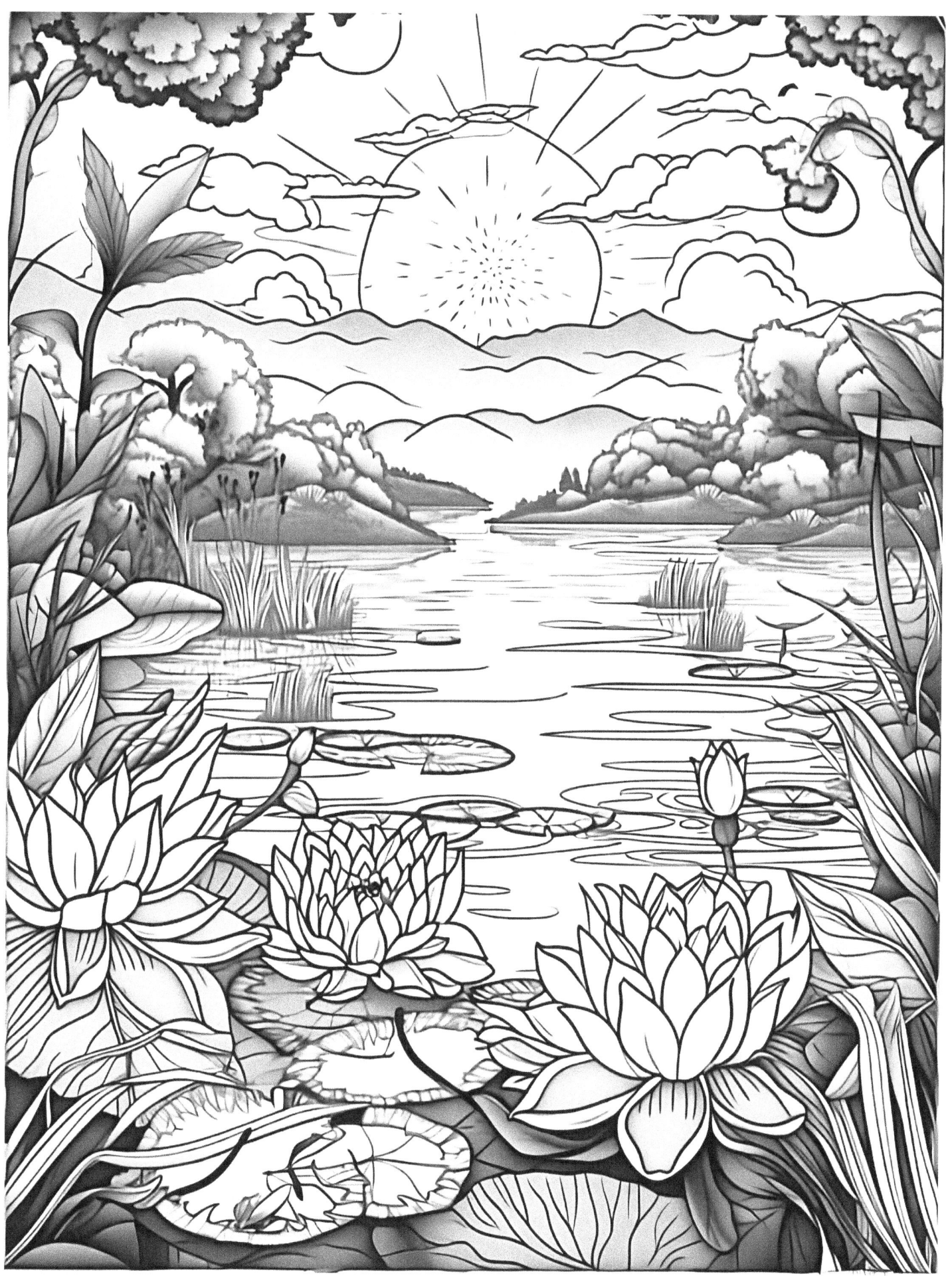

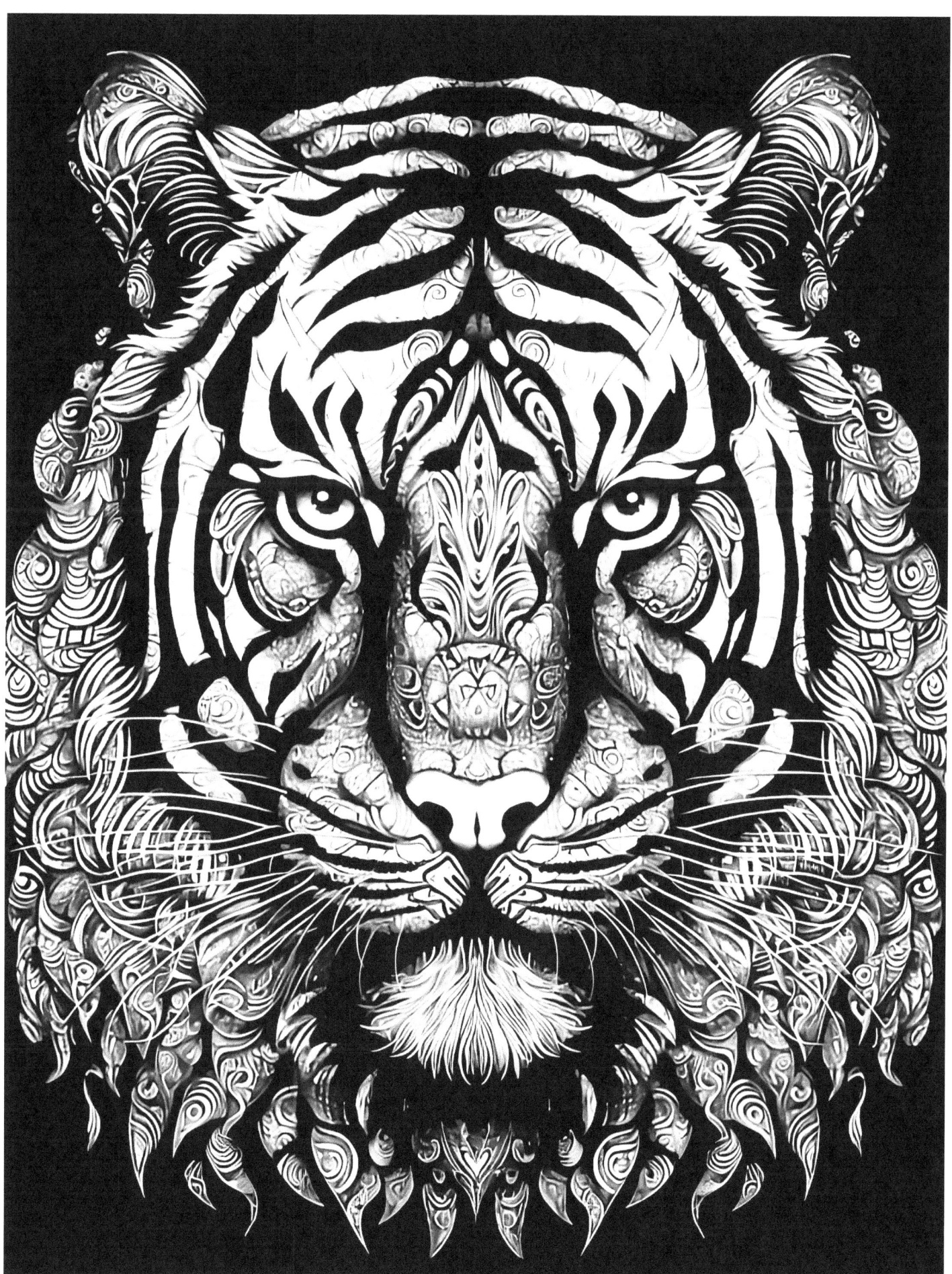

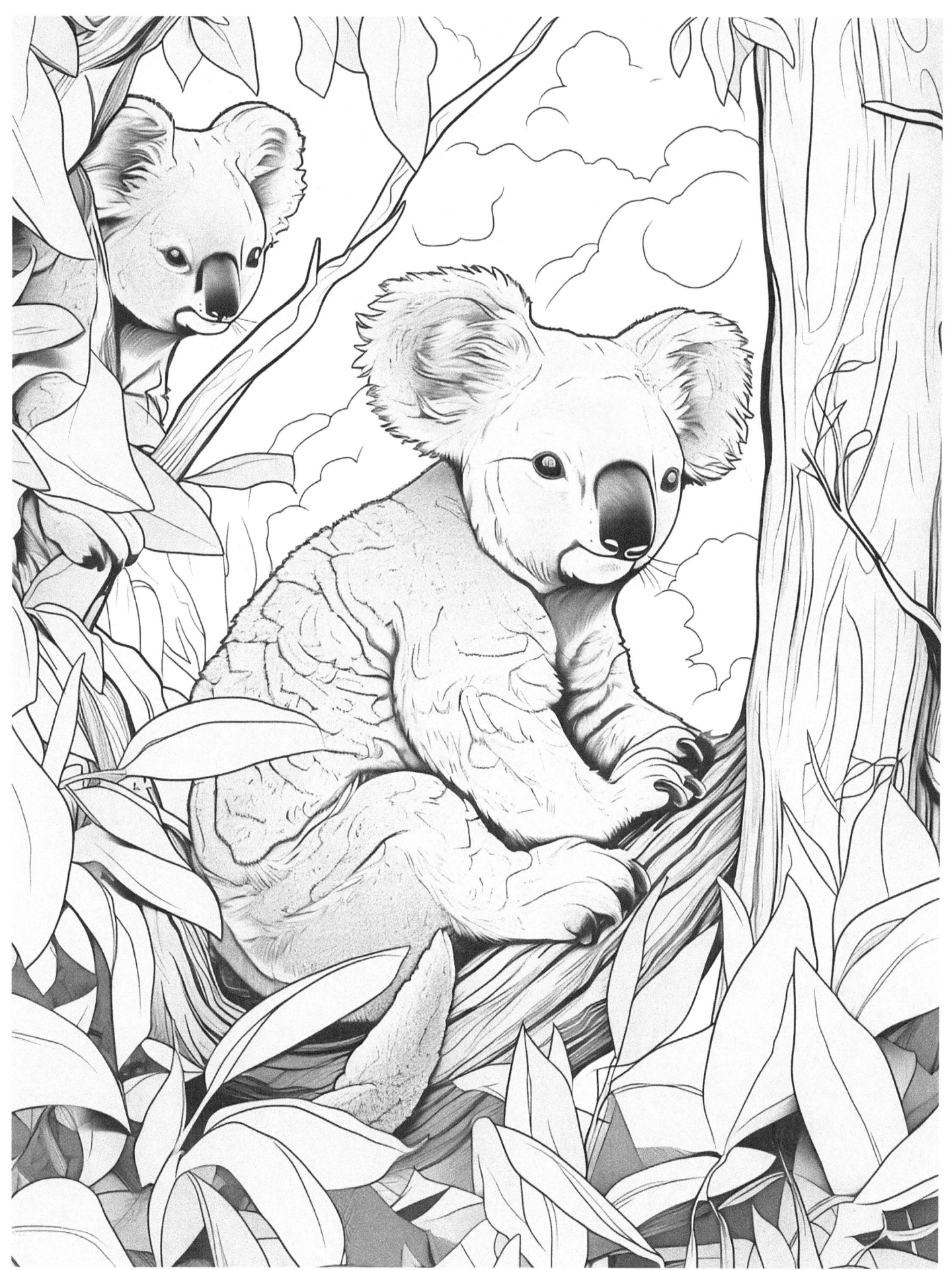

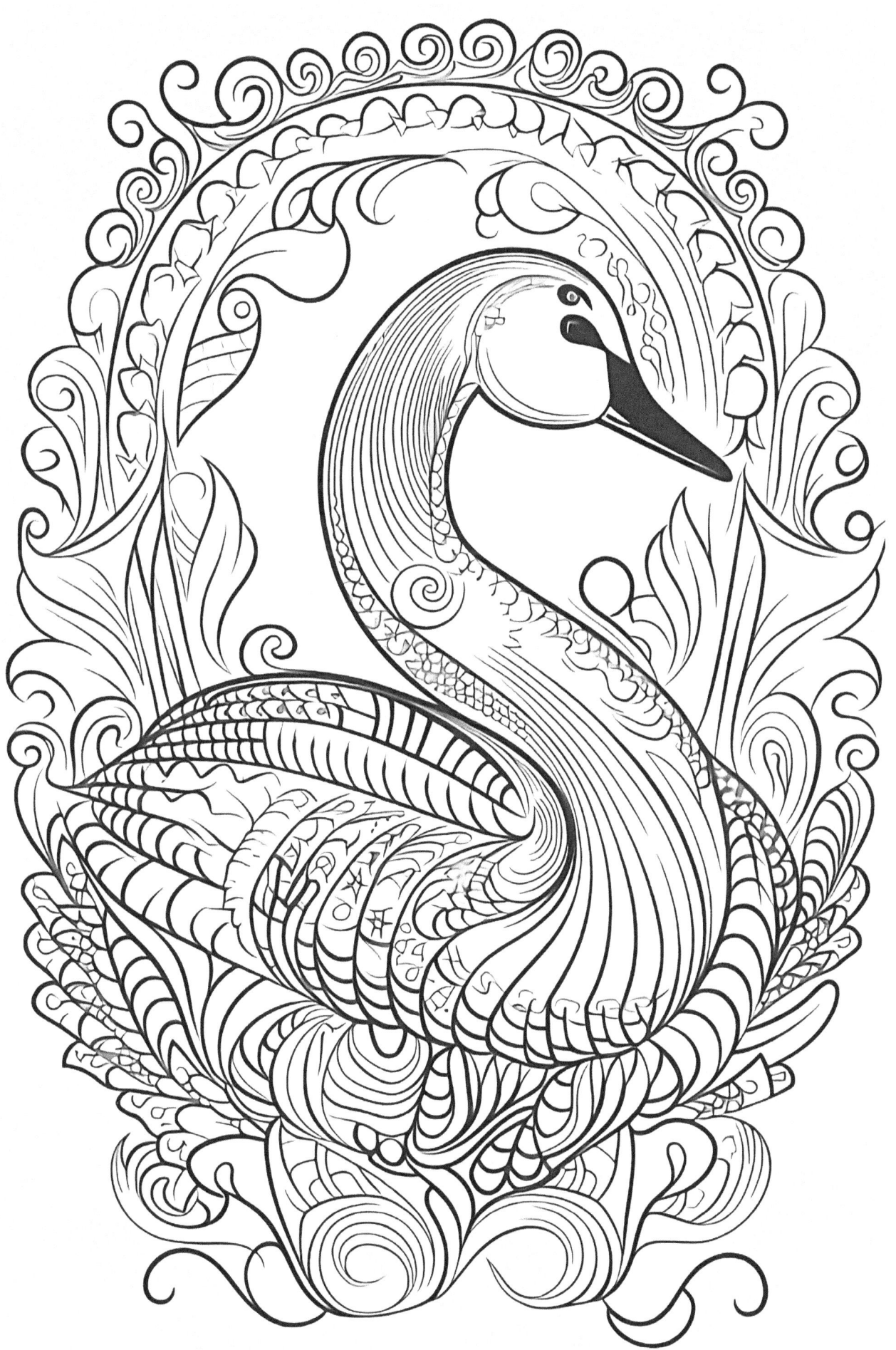

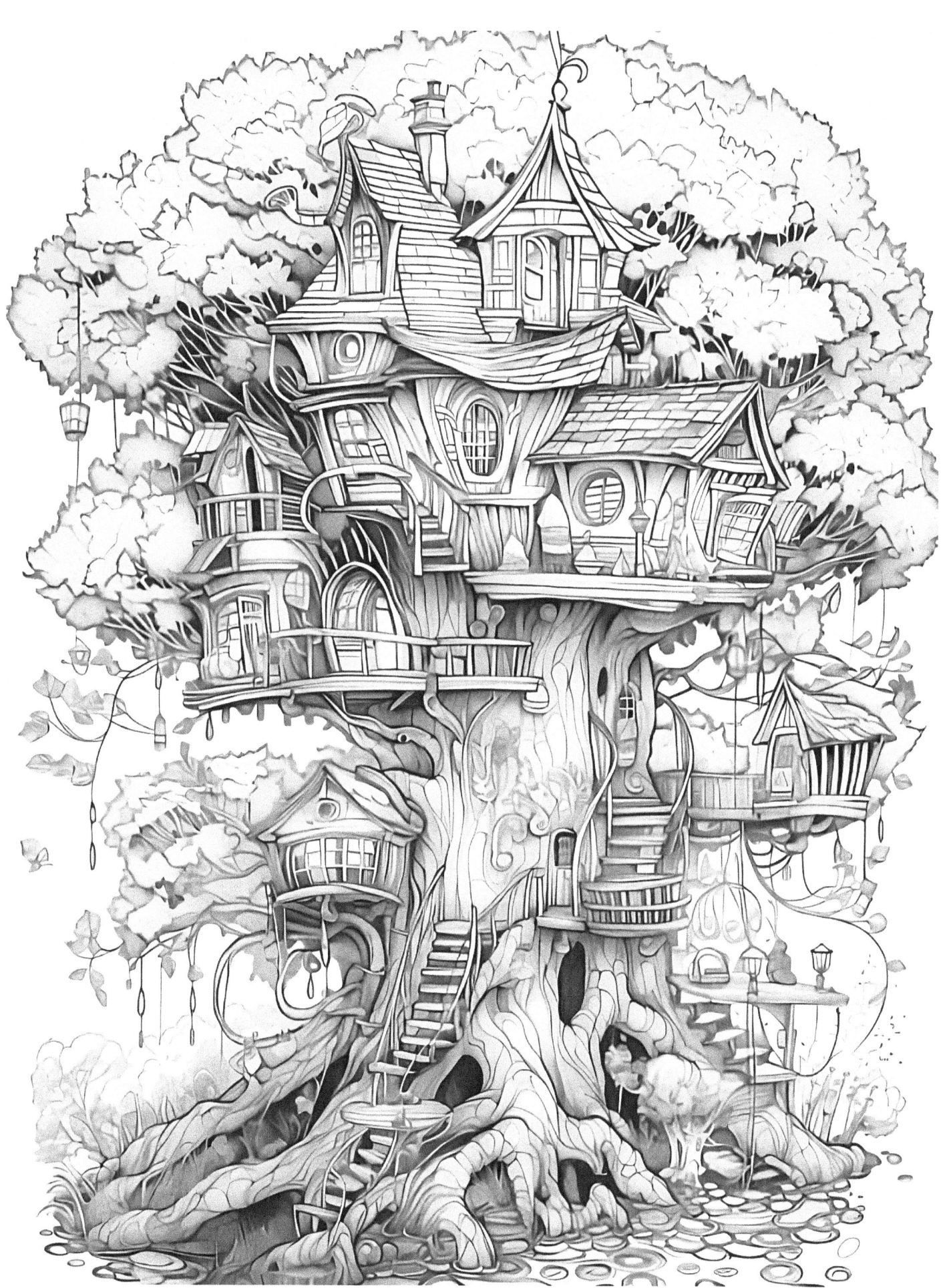

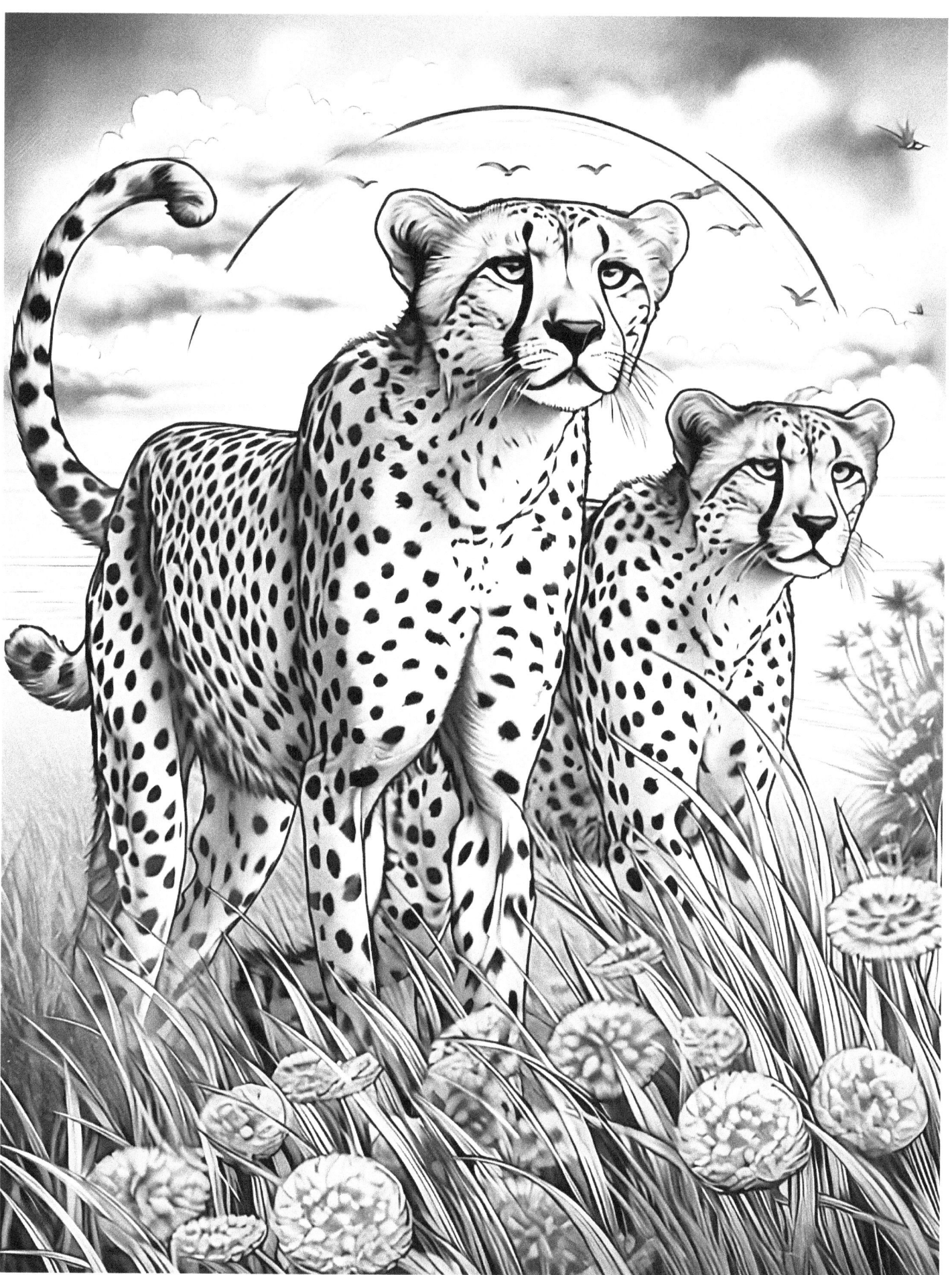

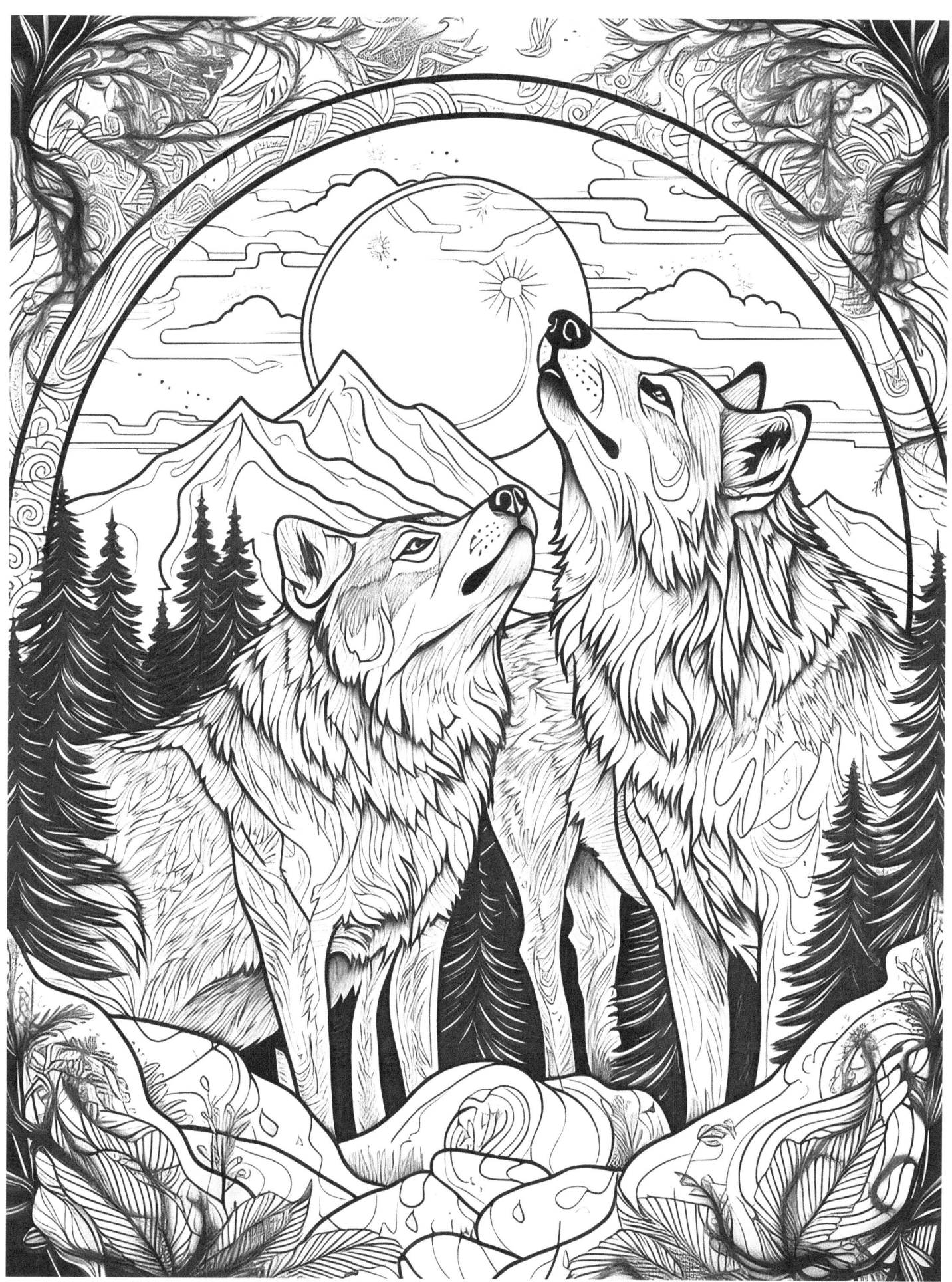

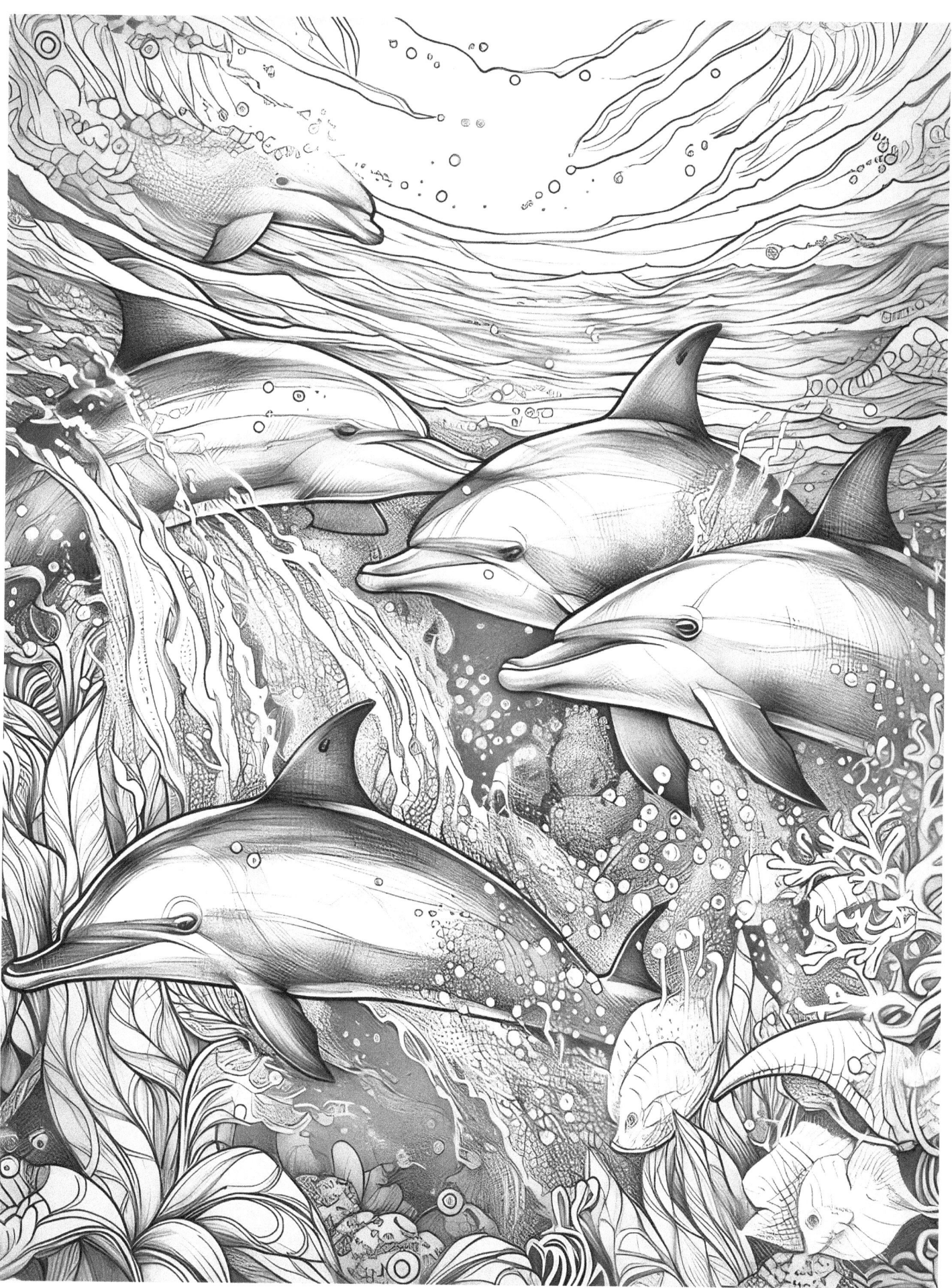

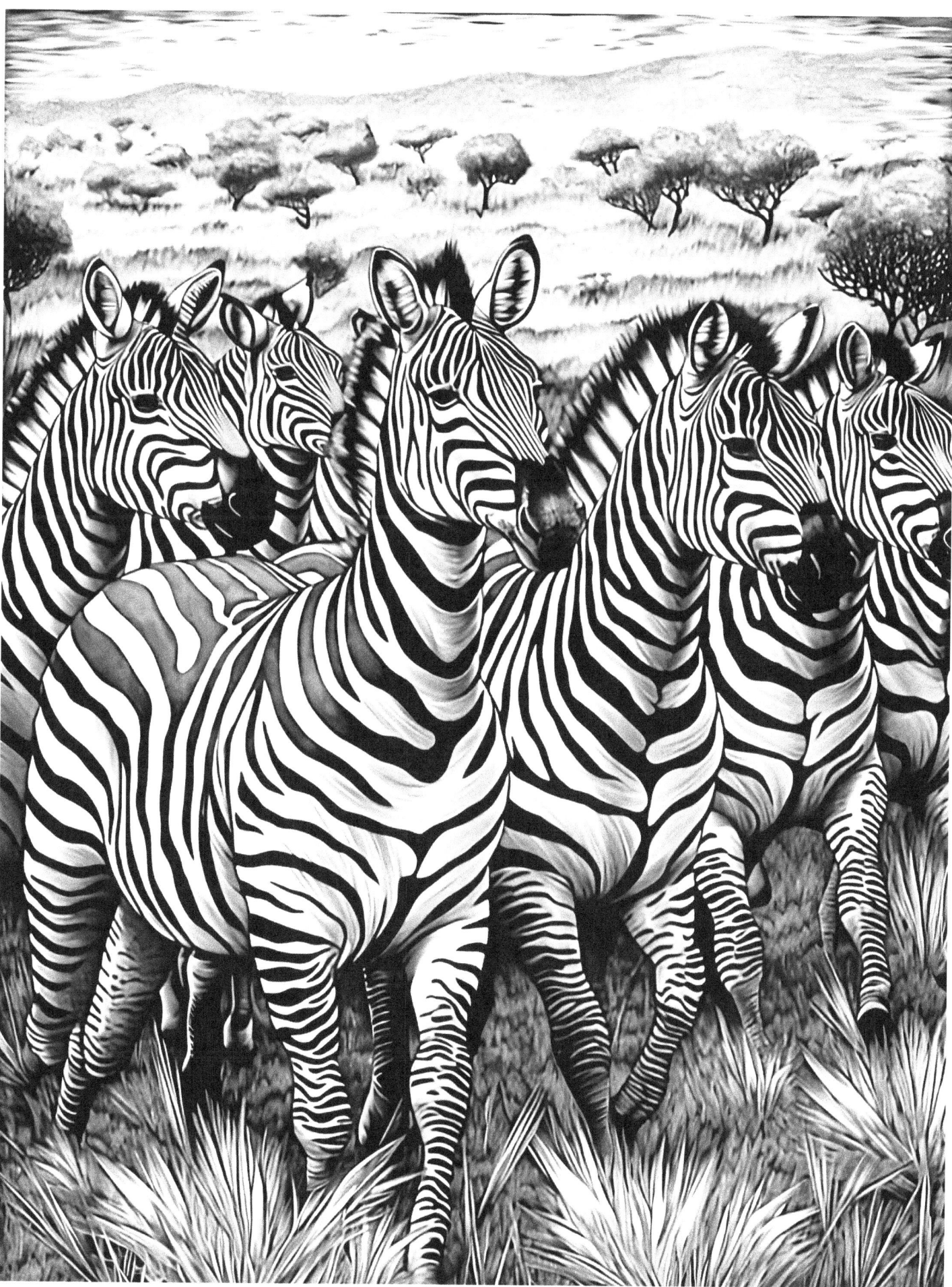

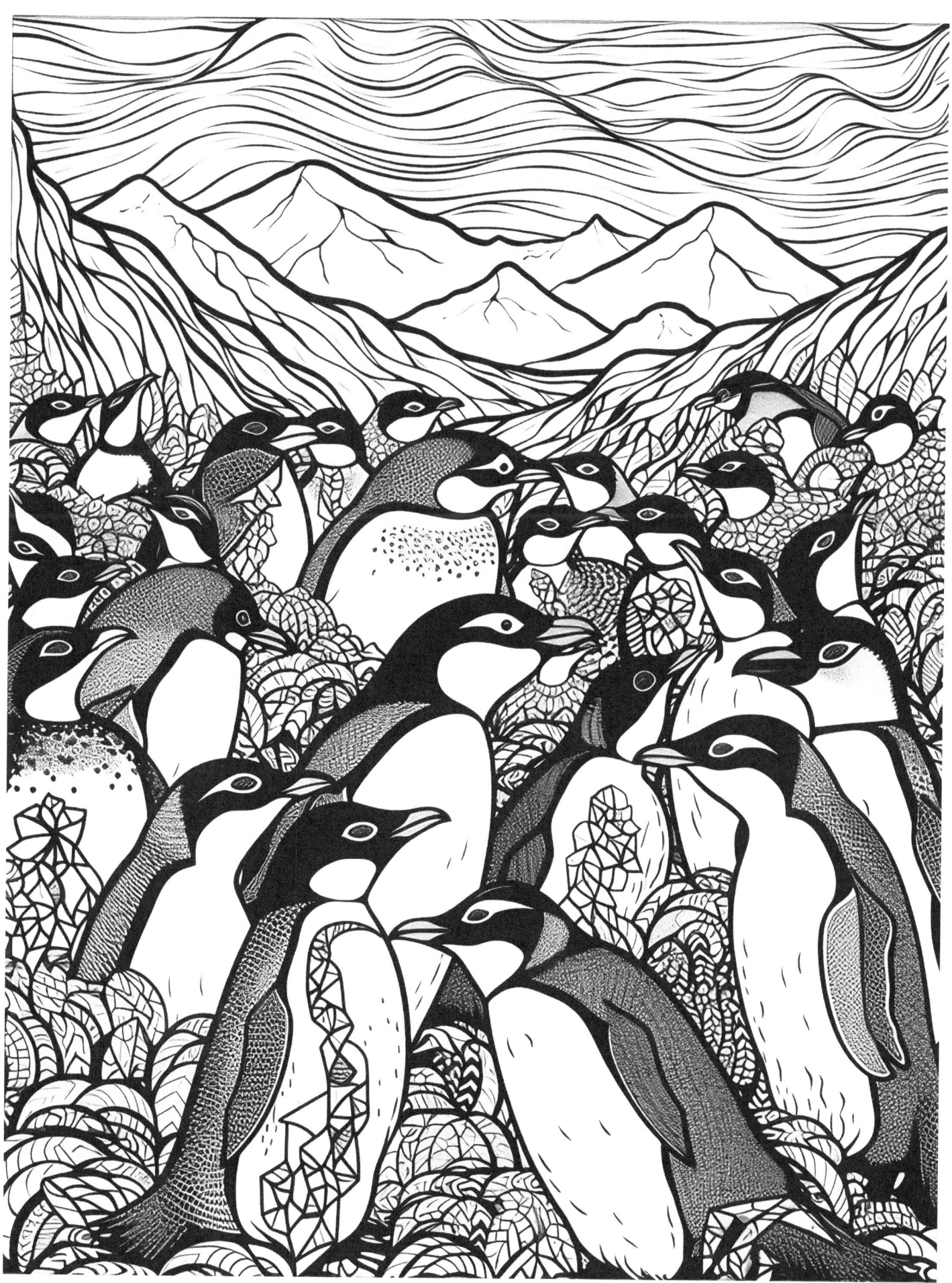

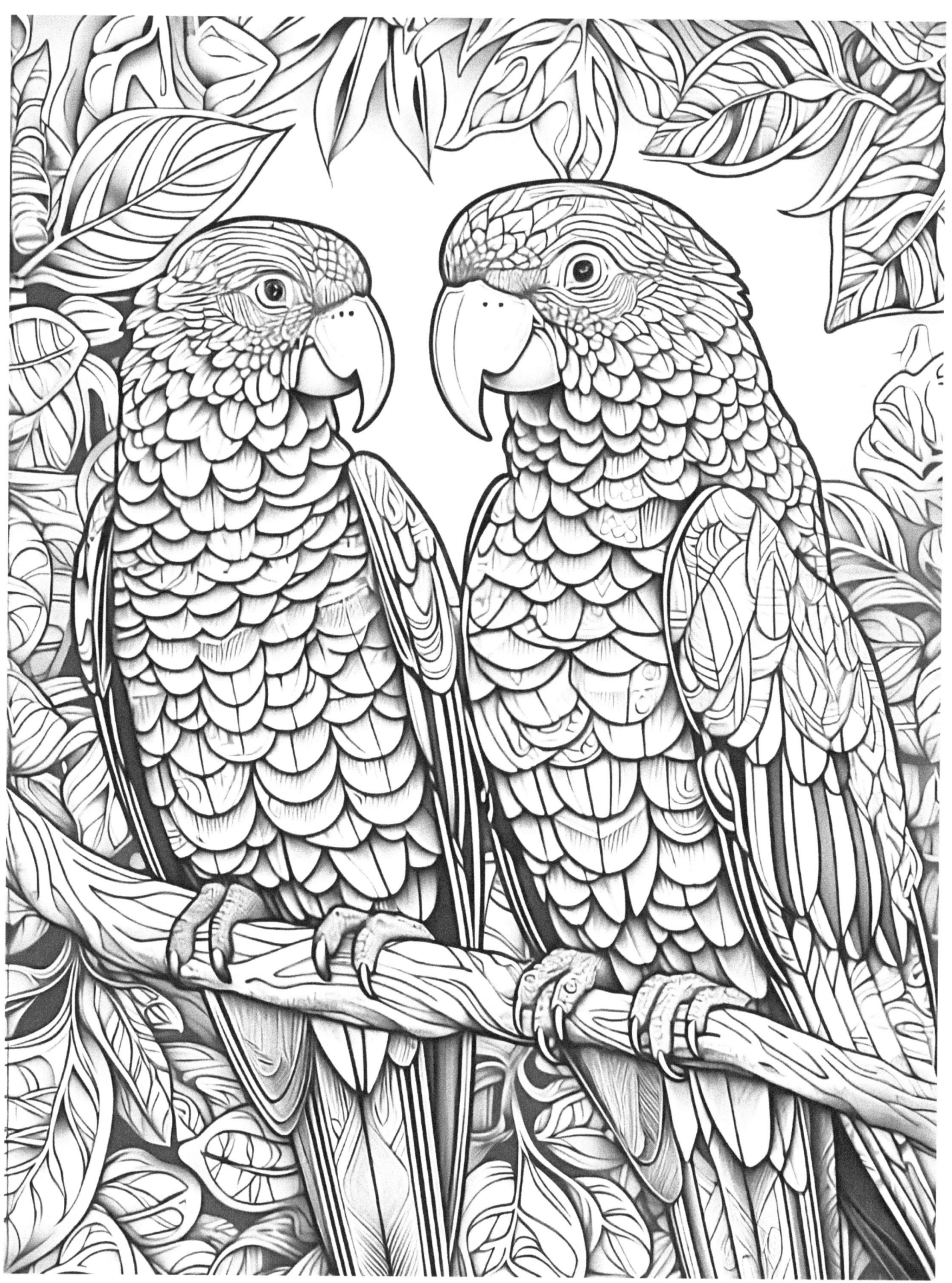

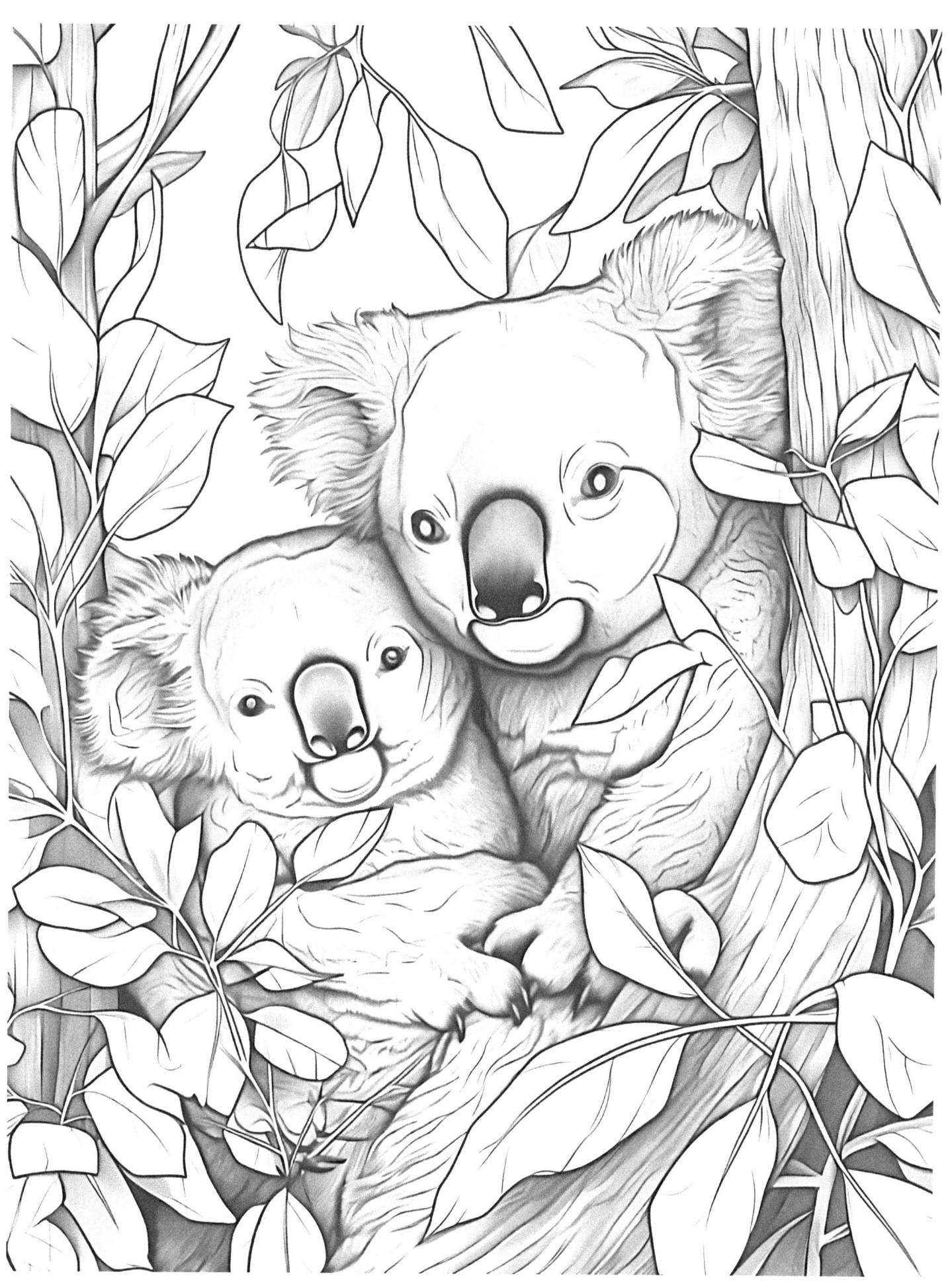

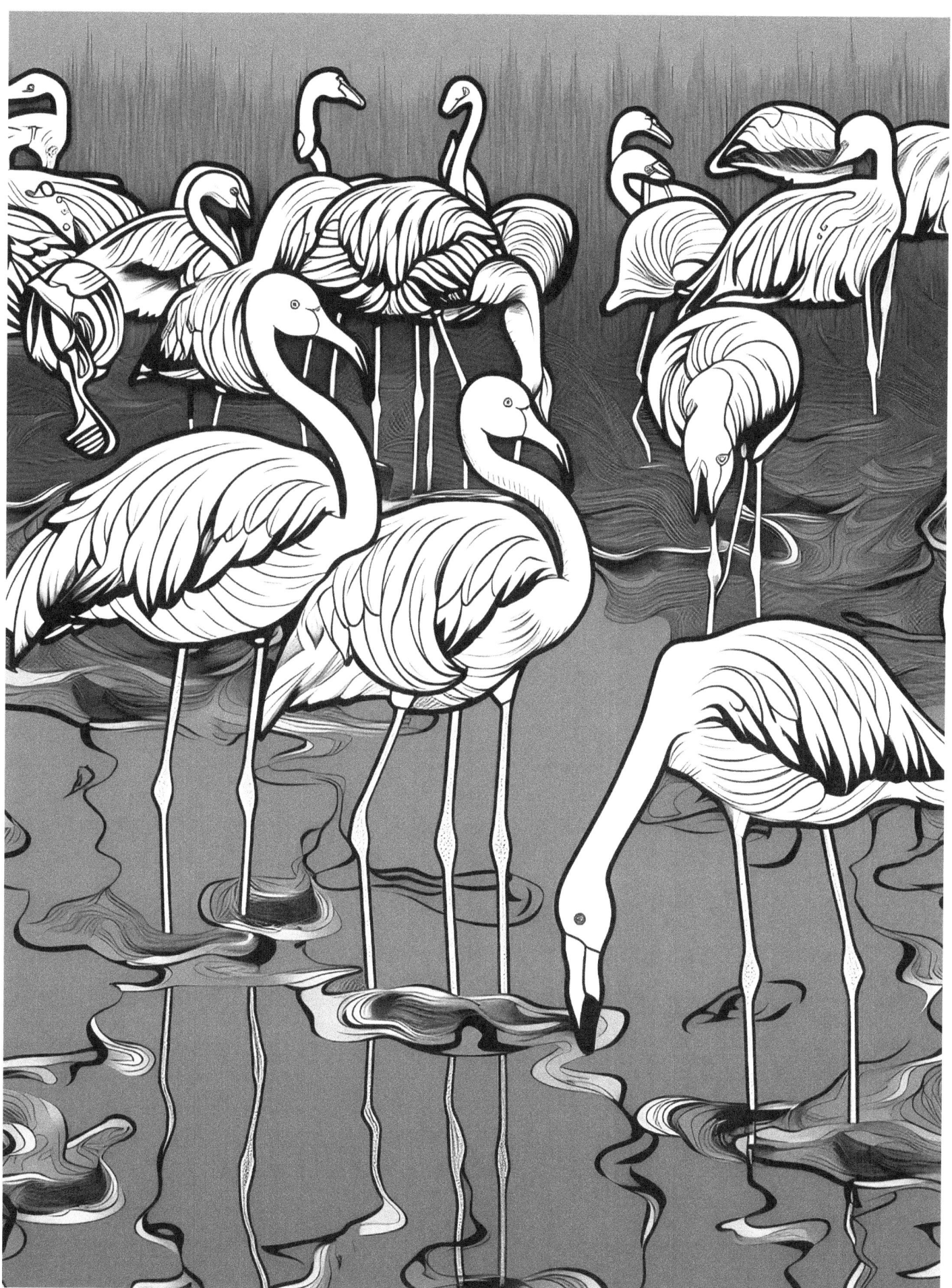

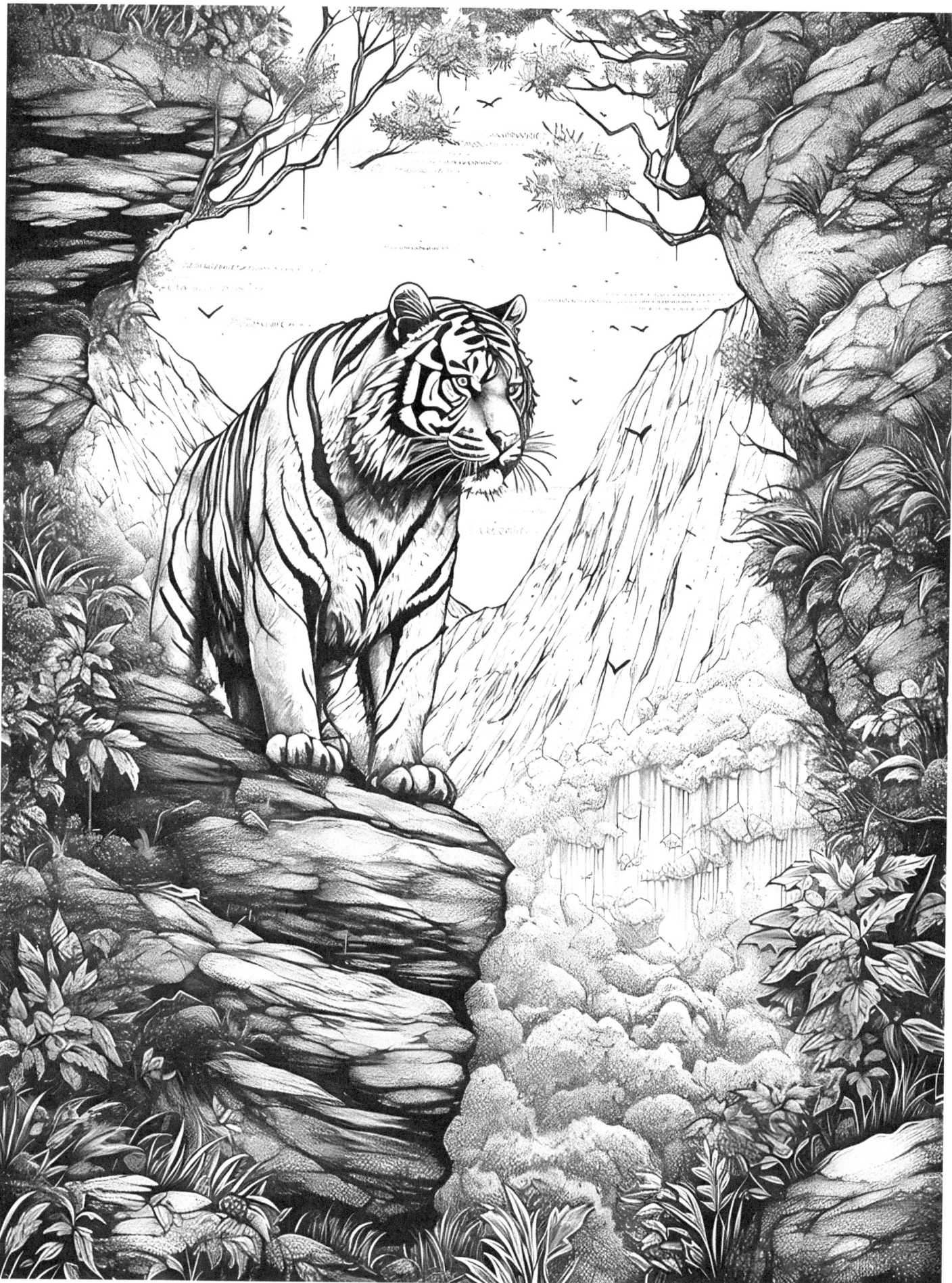

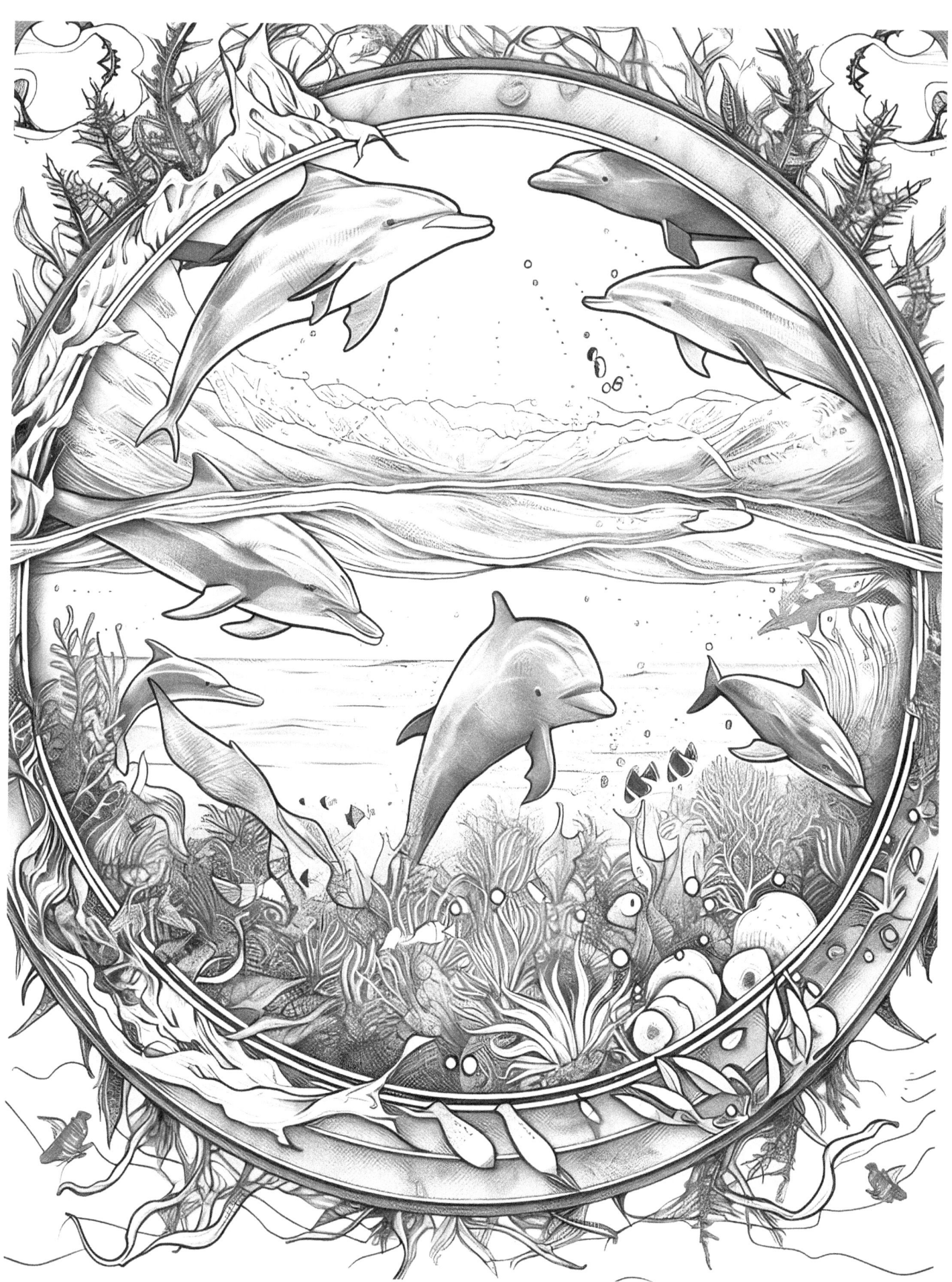

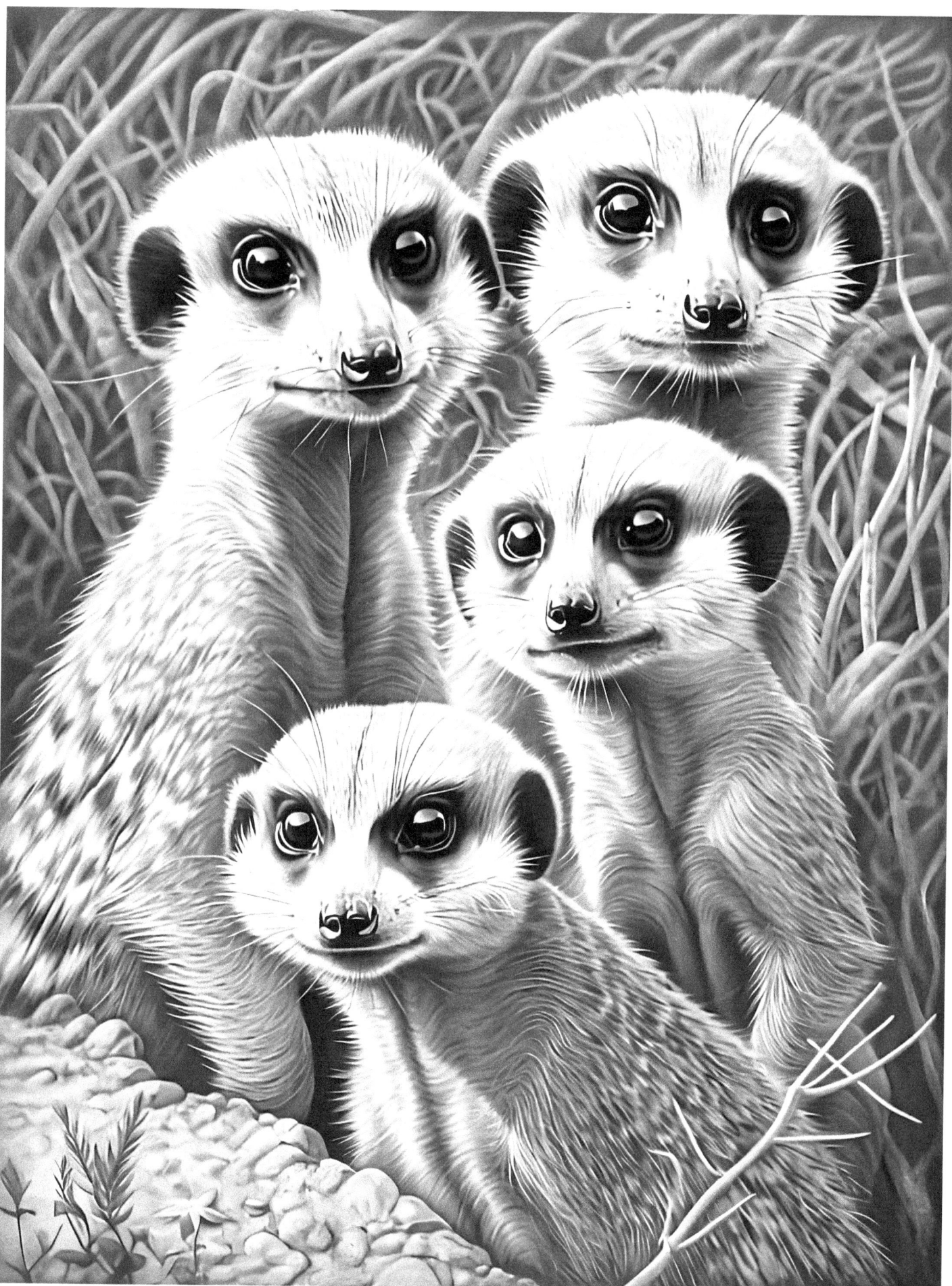

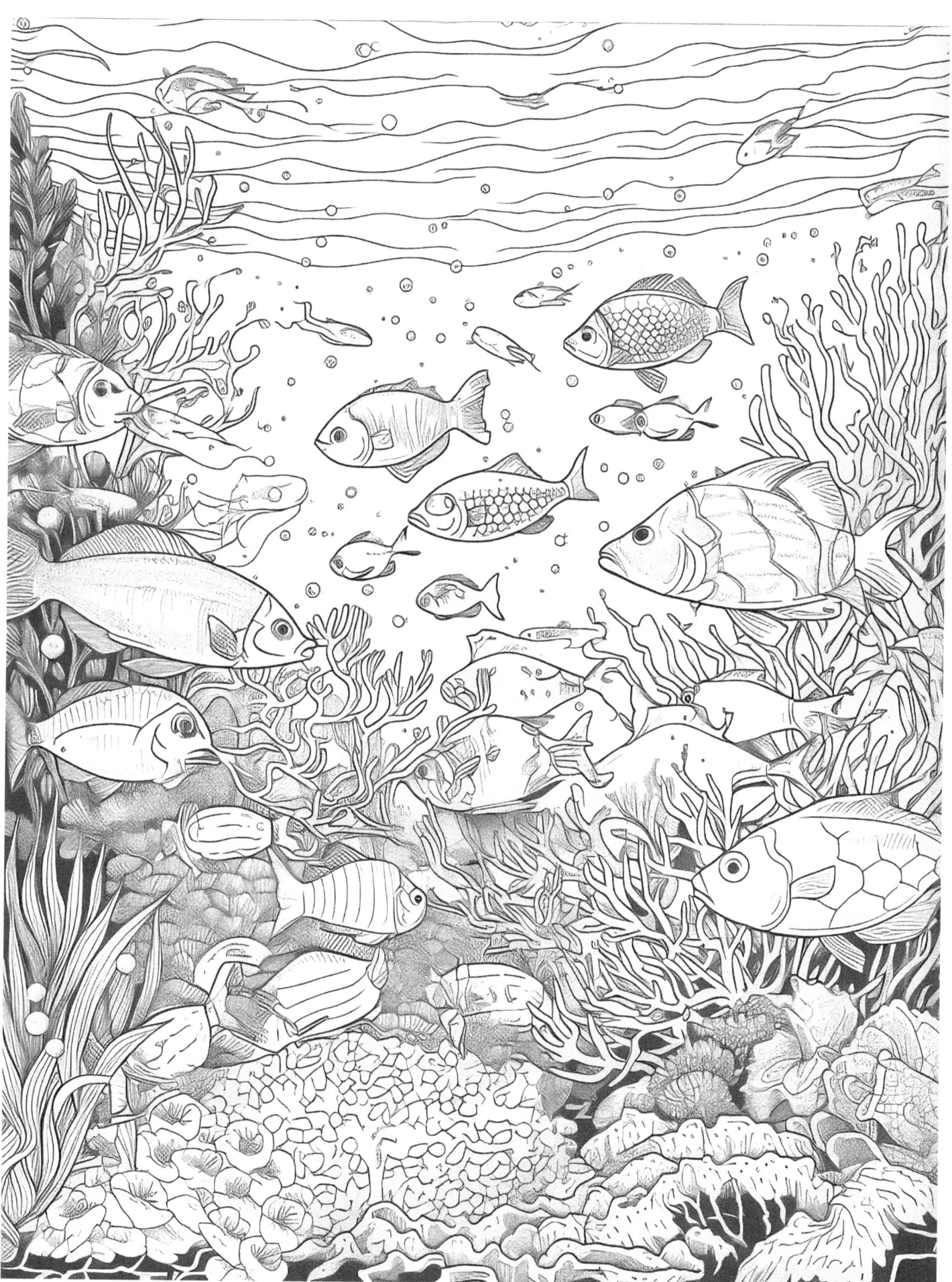

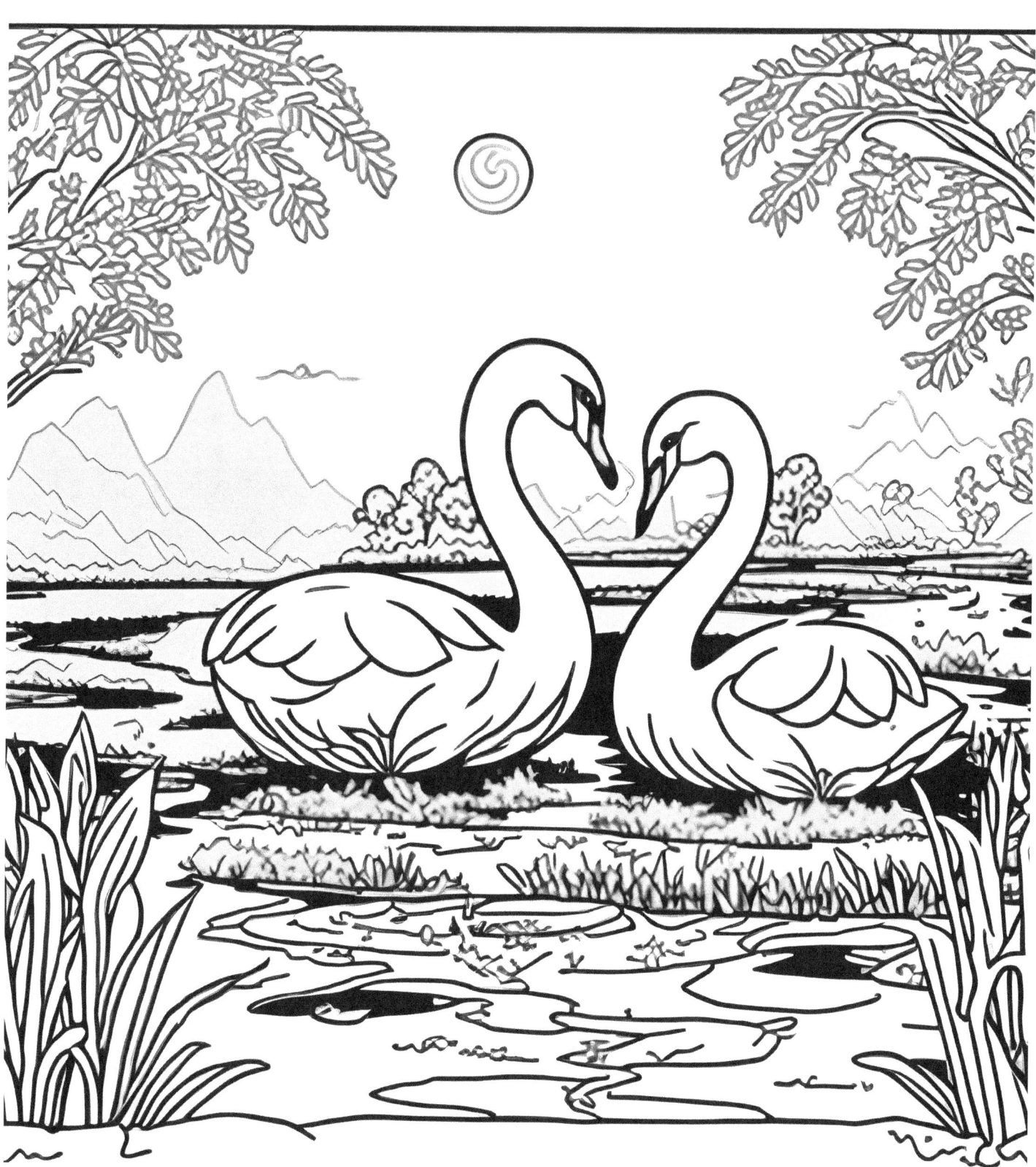

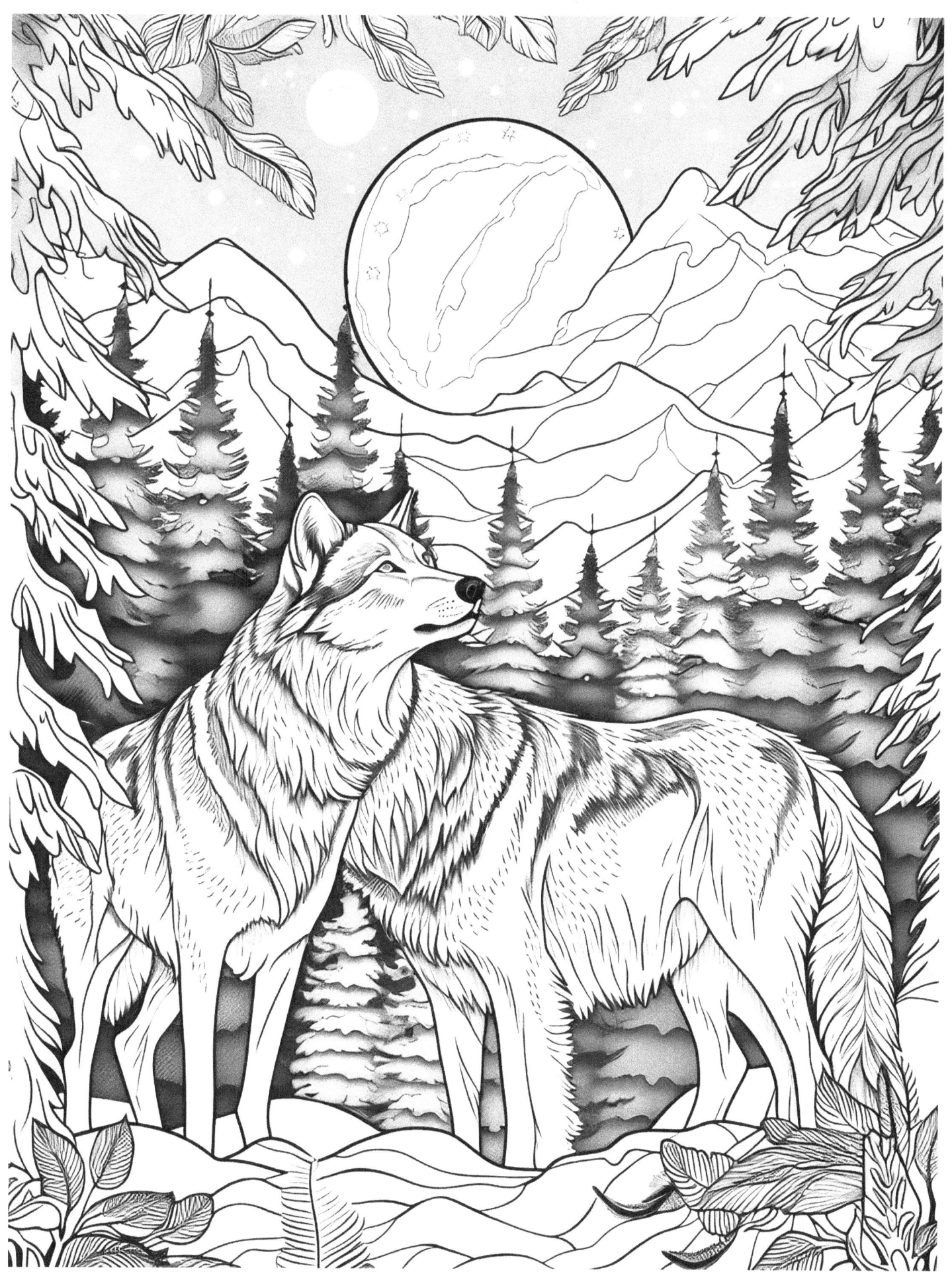

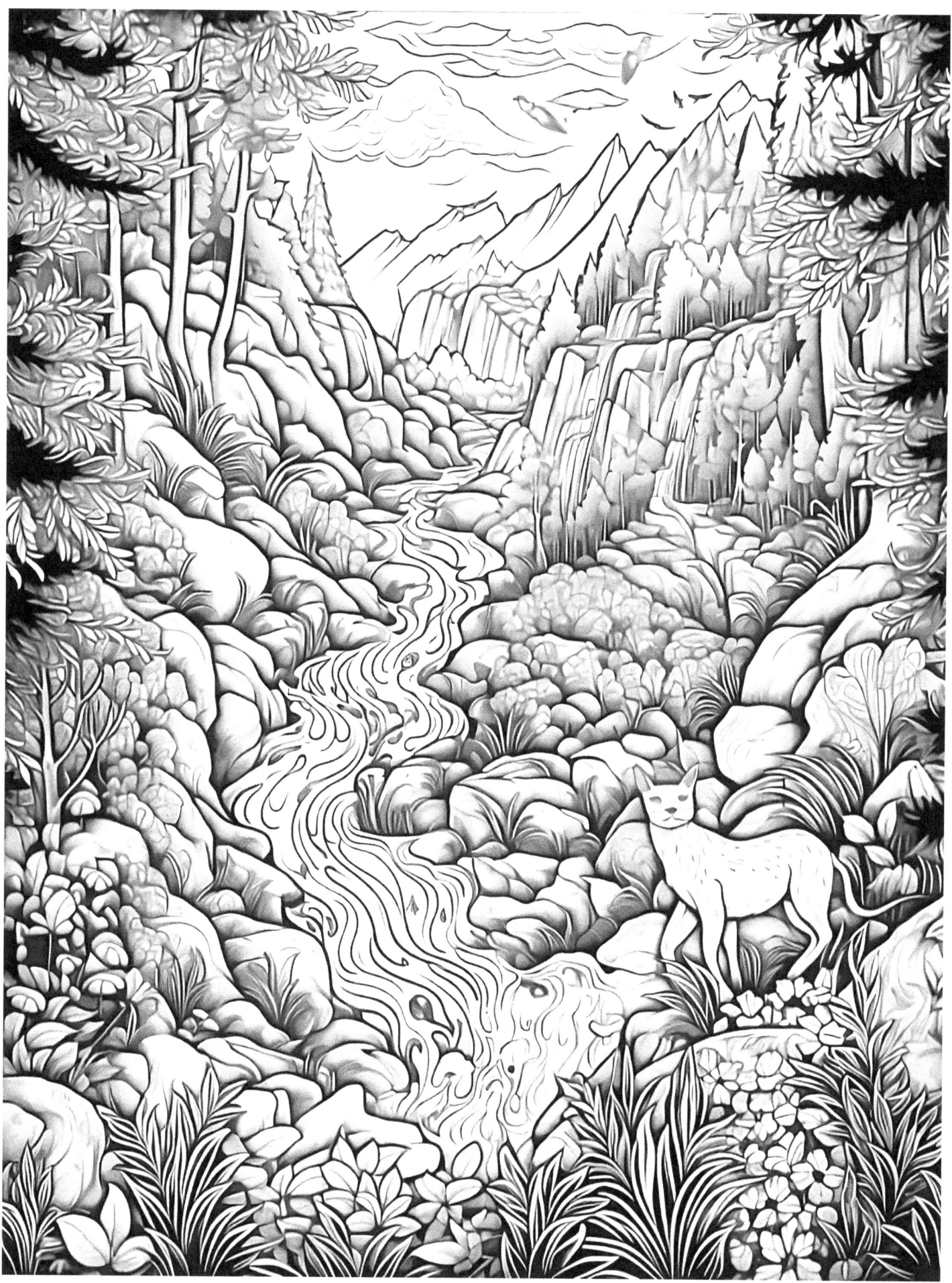

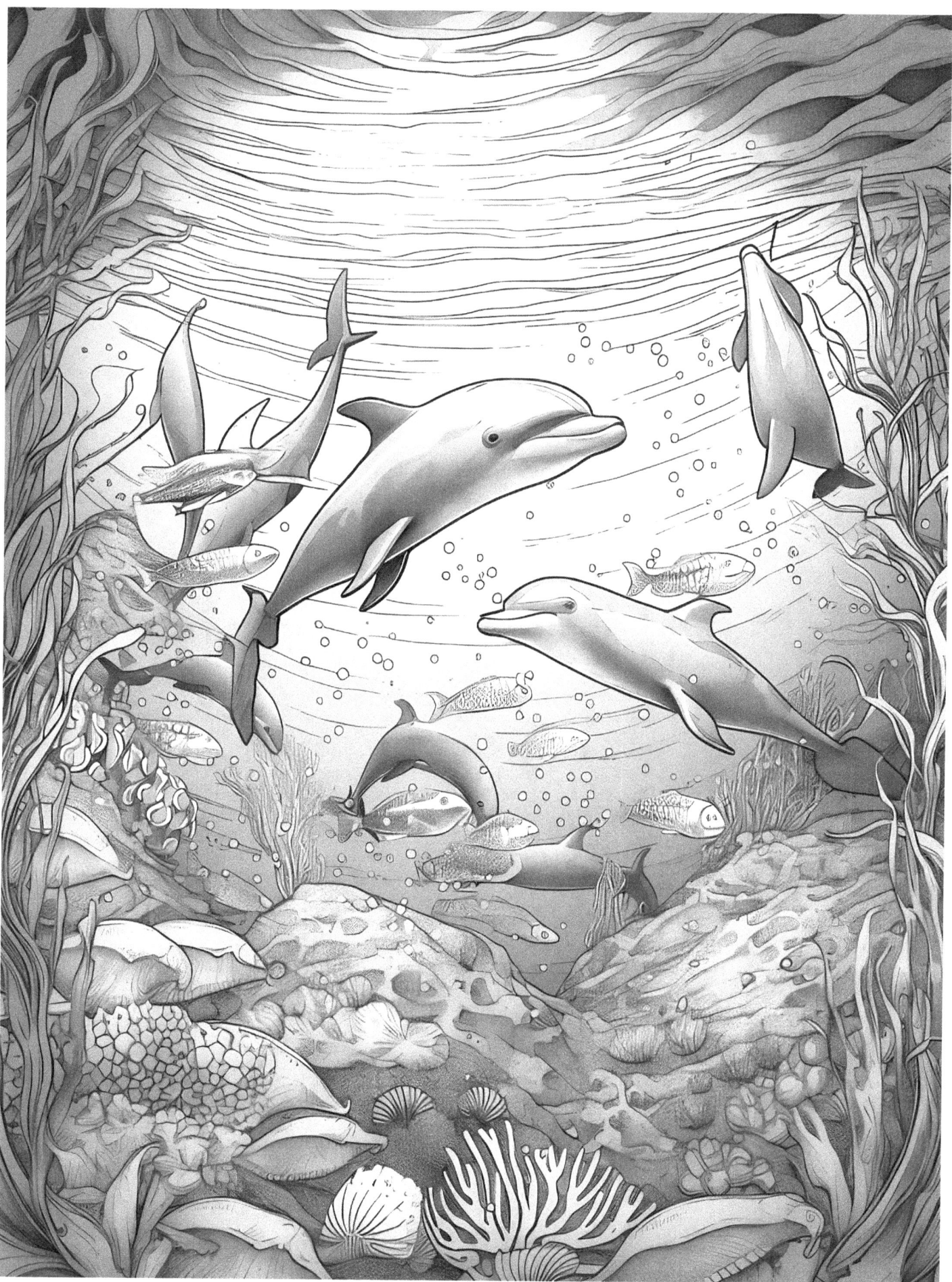

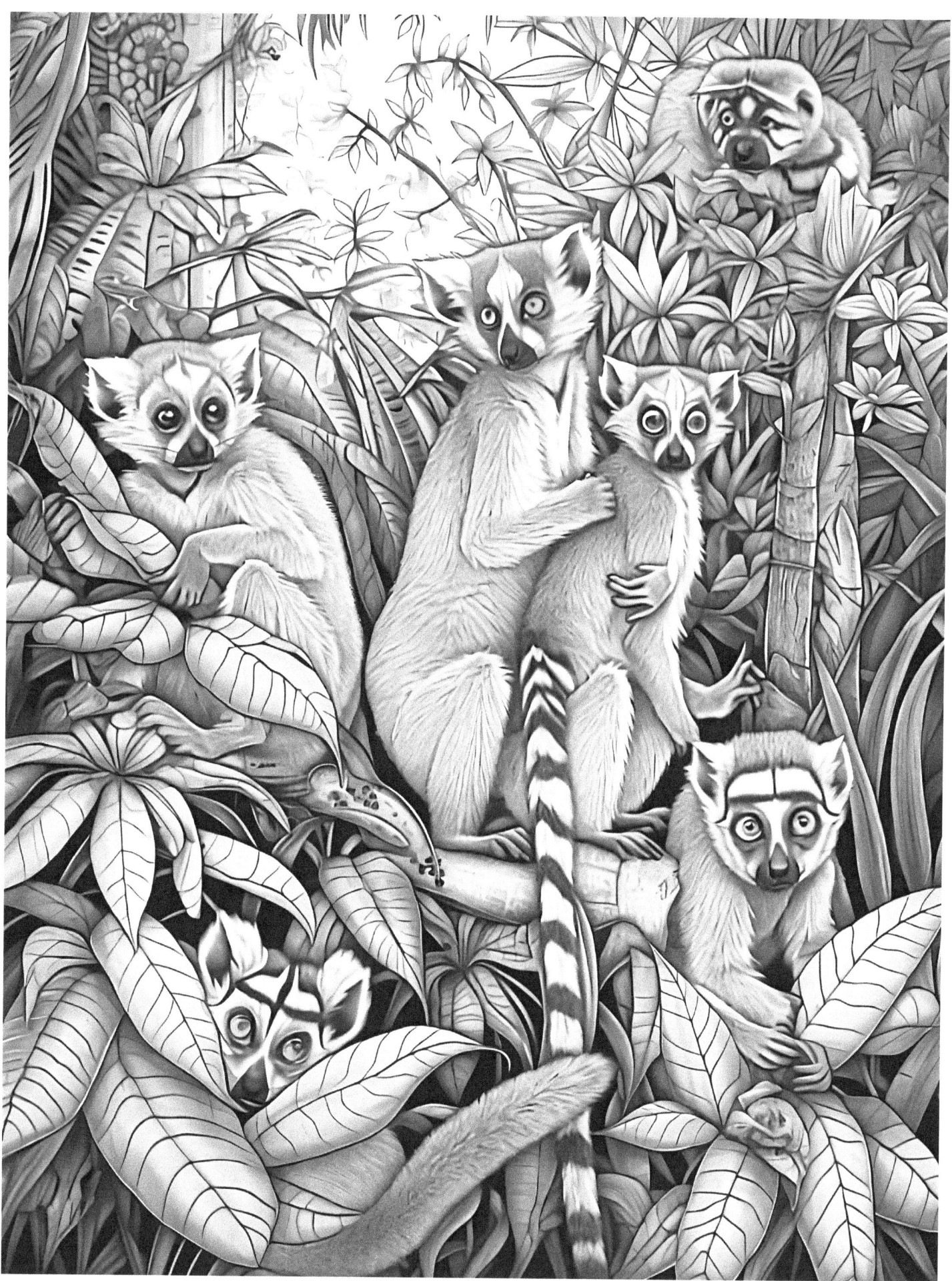

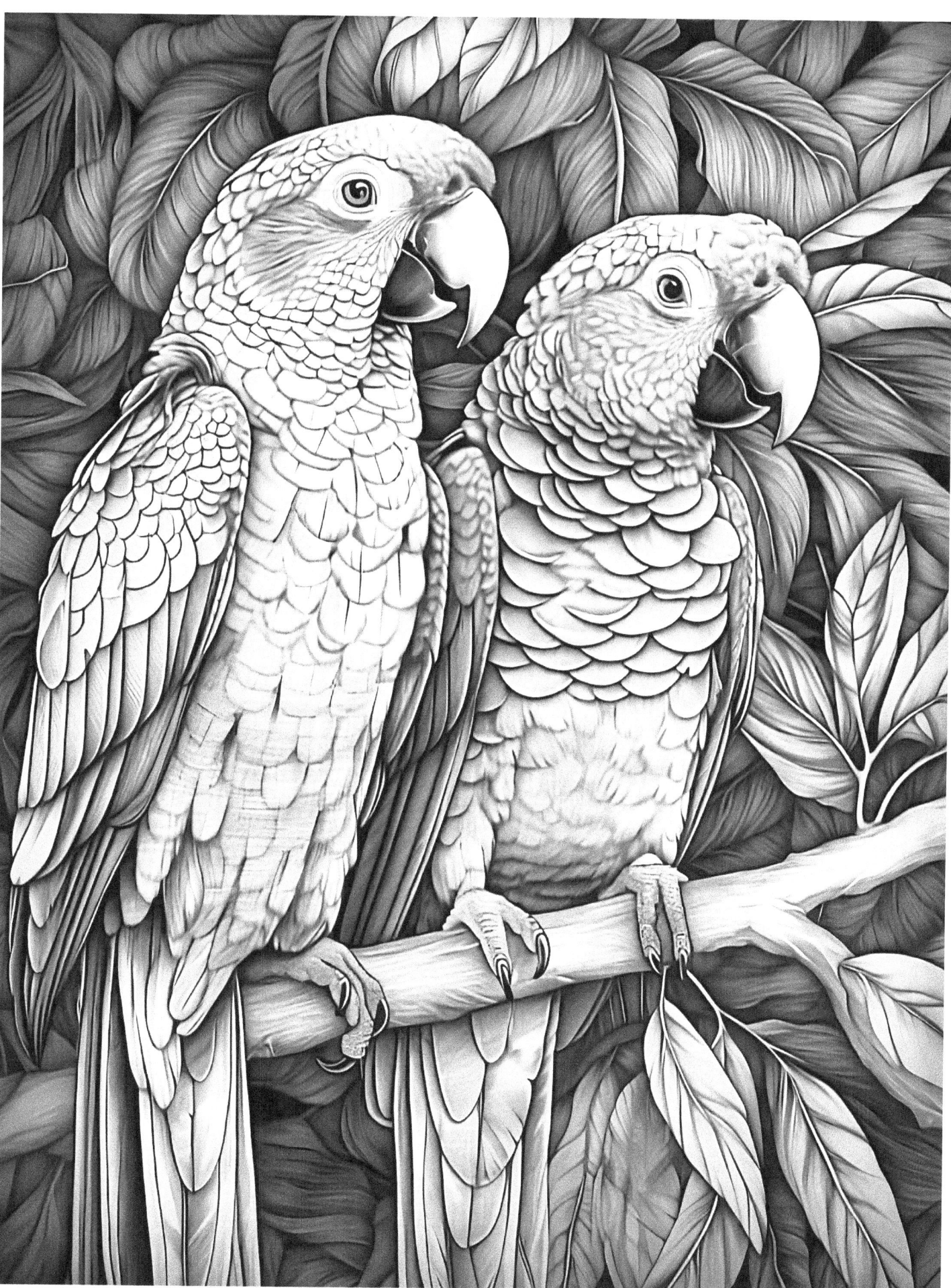

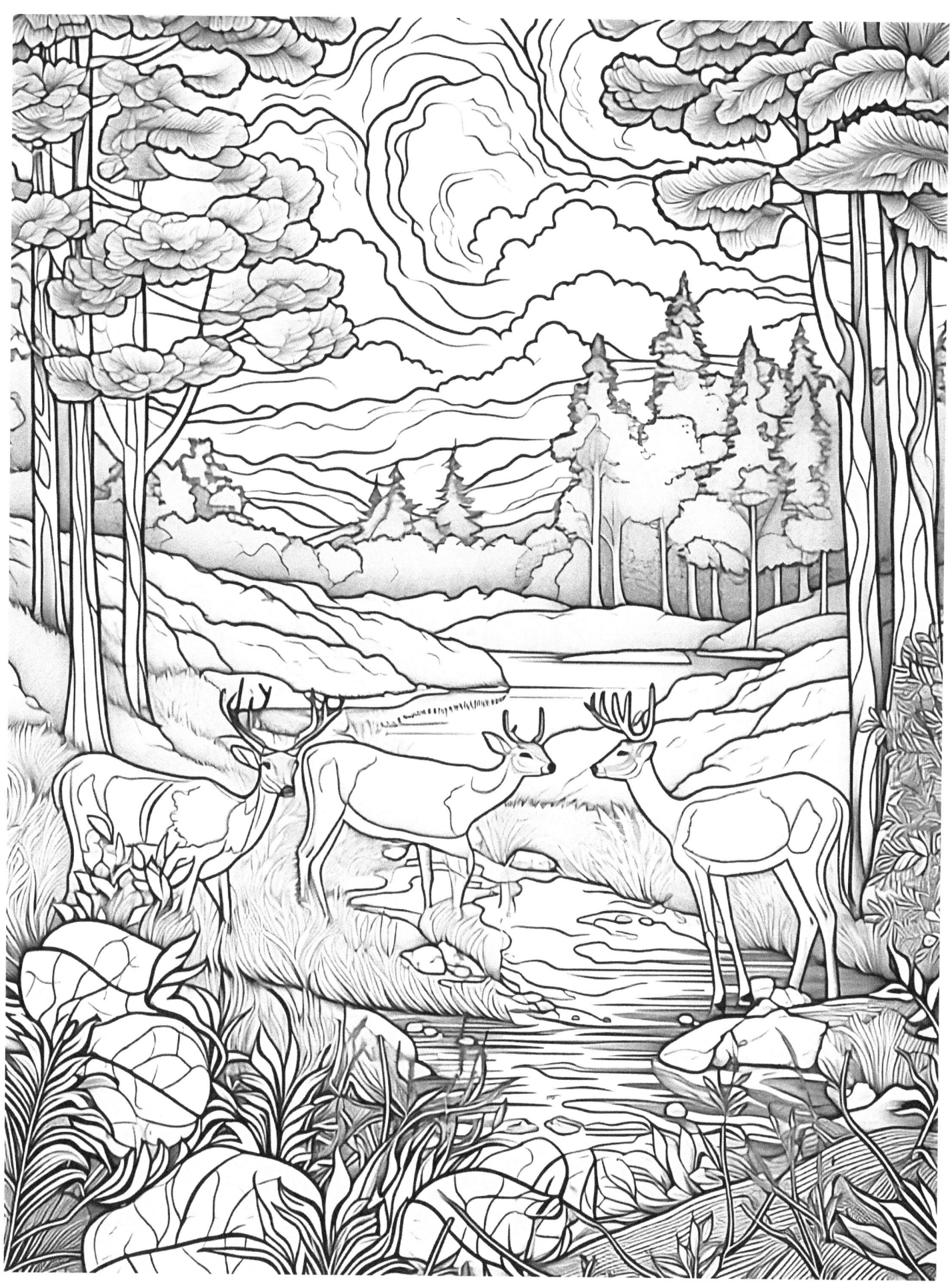

Conclusion:

We hope you have enjoyed this coloring adventure through the Enchanted Forest. By coloring these pages, we hope you have been able to unwind, relax, and connect with nature in a unique way. Remember to take some time out of your busy schedule to enjoy the beauty of the natural world around you. Happy coloring!

Thank you: On behalf of the author A.J., we want to express our gratitude for choosing this coloring book and taking the time to color through the pages. We hope this book has brought you joy and relaxation, and we appreciate your support. Thank you for taking this journey through the Enchanted Forest with us.

www.ingramcontent.com/pod-product-compliance
Lightning Source LLC
Chambersburg PA
CBHW081711220526
45467CB00034B/2493